# Glove Story
# Fathers, Sons and
# the American Pastime

Mark Rosenman and A. J. Carter

Michael,
Hope you Enjoy the Book.
Never Stop Loving the great
game of Baseball
2019

Press Box Publishing

# DEDICATION

To Morris Rosenman, Josh Rosenman, the 1,075 men who have played for the New York Mets, Bob Murphy, Ralph Kiner, Lindsey Nelson, Gary Cohen, Howie Rose, and the Commack Cougars, who all have contributed to my love of baseball, and to Beth and Liana Rosenman, who tolerate my obsession for the game.

*Mark Rosenman*

To my sons, Douglas and Evan, who happily embraced their father's love of baseball, and my wife, Eileen, who allowed baseball to commandeer the den television and the dinner conversation.

*A.J. Carter*

# FOREWORD

A memory from nearly 47 years ago, and yet it seems like only yesterday.

My father, Marty Brennaman, had been named the radio voice of the Cincinnati Reds.

It was March of 1974.

Our family lived in Virginia Beach, Virginia, at the time and we probably couldn't find Cincinnati, Ohio, on a map.

But I knew it was going to be our new home within two months.

Spring training for the Reds was in Tampa, Florida . . . yet another place we'd only heard about, but never been to.

Then, in March, we went . . . my Dad and me, headed to Florida.

On that first day, at ten years young, walking into the Reds clubhouse was terrifying.

There stood men you'd only seen on TV and they were on the tube a lot . . . everywhere.

These were the Cincinnati Reds of the 1970s.

I'd always thought my Dad was a big deal while broadcasting in the minor leagues but THIS was the MAJOR LEAGUES.

Here stood Johnny Bench and Pete Rose and Joe Morgan and Sparky Anderson ... are you kidding me? I'm in the same room with these guys?

Dad calmly and confidently took me by the hand and introduced me to Rose, Morgan, Tony Perez, and and David Concepcion . . . each of the four handed me a ball and a bat.

FOUR BATS AND FOUR BALLS from those guys!

Every kid's dream who ever grew up a baseball fan.

Over the next 17 years, my Dad and I saw a lot more baseball . . . together and apart. But it was the times of going with him to sit in Sparky Anderson's office taping the pregame show, to sitting in the booth and being left at the ballpark because he thought I went home with Mom, to listening to him while in bed during a big Dodgers series from the West Coast on a summer night.

Blessed. Truly blessed.

Now I'm grateful to share those experiences with our son Luke and his sister Ella.
Whether it was coaching his baseball team or taking her to an afternoon game and skipping school, there's something about baseball, kids, and their Dads.

Others' stories are far better than ours but it's always the same ending . . . the way you feel with Dad, or Mom, watching baseball on a magical summer night.

*Thom Brennaman*

With all due respect to other sports, none can equal the great game of baseball when it comes to creating a bond between father and son. I can speak from experience because of the game we are both involved in and what it has meant to our relationship. You'll be reading in this long-overdue book about fathers and sons building a stronger bond on the playing field. The bond between Thom and me is a bit different because it's come from both broadcasting Cincinnati Reds baseball; Thom on the TV side and me on radio. Over the years, being together virtually every day during each season has brought us closer than it ever was before.

It's become a truly special bond with my only son and I'll forever be thankful for it. In this book you're going to read many more like it. Enjoy!

*Marty  Brennaman*

The Brennamans, Marty and Thom,the Radio and TV voices of the Cincinnati Reds.
(Photo courtesy the Cincinnati Reds.)

# CONTENTS

# ACKNOWLEDGMENTS

## MARK'S ACKNOWLEDGEMENTS

Over the course of my lifetime I have read thousands of books. I, like many others, do not always take the time to read the Acknowledgments. Having gone through the process of writing a book for the fifth time, I truly now understand how important these pages are to the pages that follow, for without the names I am about to list, this book would not exist.

First and foremost, as always, is my amazing wife, Beth, who is always there as an endless source of encouragement and support. My son, Josh, his finance Stefania, and my daughter, Liana, who by the way they approach everything they do in life with such passion inspires me to do the same.

My late parents, Morris and Estelle, allowed be to buy every sports book whenever there was a book fair at school and always encouraged me to pursue my passions.

My late sisters, Cheryl and Suzie, who always set great examples for their little brother.

Heartfelt gratitude goes out to my Little League coaches Connie Ring and Frank Santoriello, as well as my high school coaches, Greg McArthur and Joe DiMaggio (not that Joe DiMaggio), who gave so much of their time and imparted a love of the game in so many.

I would like to thank the following members of the press who welcomed me into their working place with open arms and showed me the ropes, including Ken Albert ,Christian Arnold, Larry Brooks, Matt Calamia, Rick "Carpy" Carpinello, Jim Cerny, Tina Cervasio, Scott Charles, Gary Cohen, Russ Cohen, Ed Coleman, Rich Coutinho, Charles Curtis, Brett Cyrgalis, Nelson Figueroa, Bob Gelb, Zach Gelb, Steve Gelbs, John Giannone, Denis Gorman, Andrew Gross, Sean Hartnett, Howie Karpin, Patrick Kearns, Kevin Kernan, Allan Kreda, Don La Greca, David Lennon, Pat Leonard, Josh Lewin, Dave Maloney, Mike Mancuso, Gil Martin, Joe McDonald, Joe Micheletti, Brian Monzo, Steve Overmyer, Ira Podell, Ed Randall, Howie Rose, Sam Rosen, Seth Rothman, Adam Rubin, Ashley Sarge, Arthur Staple, Chayim Tauber, and Steve Zipay.

I have been blessed by having Jiggs McDonald, Tim McCarver, Ken Albert, and Dave Maloney provide forewords to my previous books. I was thrilled when Marty and Thom Brennaman agreed to write the foreword to Glove Story. They are a perfect example of what this book is all about.

I appreciate the insight that Ken Griffey Sr, Tim Raines Sr., Brian McRae, Dick Schofield, Ruben Amaro Jr., Maury and Bump Wills, Tim and Chad Wallach, Ed and Bobby Crosby, Don and Damon Buford, David Bell, Bret Boone, Mark Carreon, Mark Leiter, Mookie Wilson, and numerous other major-league fathers and sons shared what baseball meant to each of their relationships.

Thank you to the New York Mets media relations department, Jay Horwitz, Harold Kaufman, and Ethan Wilson for all their help during this project as well as Doug Dickey for all his input and all of his amazing Mets Fantasy Camp staff for running an amazing camp.

Thank you to John Labombarda and the staff of the Elias Sports Bureau, Brendan Hader and the Cincinnati Reds communications department, Dina Blevins and the Kansas City Royals communications department, Jerry Lewis of the Detroit Tigers Fantasy Camp, Mark Stone from the LADABC Fantasy Camp, and the staff of Baltimore Orioles Dream Week for their help during this project.

Thanks to Kyle Drone of the great father-son run Dinger Bats for supplying me with the beautiful  personalized bats to use at camp.

Thank you to the WLIE 540am SportstalkNY intern Ryan Sherman, who was a huge help in transcribing hours of interviews.

A note of thanks to my SportstalkNY show sponsors Leith Baren, Neil Cohen, Gary Pincus, Andrew and David Reale, Rob Solomon, Morris Sutton, David, Victor, Ruby and Jonah Bibi, your continued support of the show is the reason this book is even possible.

A tip of the cap to Peter Golenbock, the late Phil Pepe, and George Plimpton, and Stan Fischler, who were my favorite authors growing up as well as Erik Sherman, Marty Appel, Carlo DeVito, Greg Prince, Brett Topel and the hundreds of authors who have appeared on  SportstalkNY and inspired me .

Thanks to our editor, Ken Samelson, who believed in this project from day one and saw it through to the end.

My best friend, Jeff Cohen, who I spent so many hours with at Shea Stadium, Citi Field or in front of a TV watching the Mets or talking or texting about the Mets, you are without a doubt another reason why I love the Mets.

High fives to the Sunday morning Huntington WW class. Your support helped me get in shape to survive 2019 Mets Fantasy Camp.

Kudos to Dr. Richard Weiss for his encyclopedic recall for all things Mayfair Little League.

Thanks to my hitting coach Reggie Jackson (not that Reggie Jackson), without him there was no double down the line.

Fist bumps to the 2019 Citi Slickers coaches Eric Hillman and Pete Schoreuk, and teammates Mitch Waxman, Rich Boyd, "Bobble" Ed Moore, Seth Davis, Bob Ghandi, David "Turtle" Dolgin, Bobby Whalen, Phil Forman, and Dave Helfrich for being such an amazing group of guys.

Last, but not least, my writing partner in this project, A. J. Carter, who has been there every step of the way, starting as my assistant coach with the Cougars, to co-hosting SportstalkNY, to co-authoring Glove Story, thanks for being the perfect batterymate.

## A J.'S ACKNOWLEDGEMENTS

When you write a book, especially your first book, choosing whom to acknowledge has one overriding question: Do you limit yourself only to those who assisted in the creation of this work, or do you acknowledge all who got you from the start to where you are today?

Bear with me a bit, as I have chosen the latter.

Thank you to my wife, Eileen, and my sons, Doug and Evan,

who allowed me to pursue this project, sometimes with support and sometimes with bemusement. Your comments and suggestions were incredibly valuable— Eileen, for living this with me; Evan for staying with baseball throughout your teenage years as your "alternate sport," and Doug for being my sounding board as you patiently let me read passages aloud as I was writing this book.

Thank you to my parents, Anita and Norman Carter, who were the yin and yang muses of this project: one, my father, for whom sports formed a significant part of his adult life, albeit as a referee; the other, my mother, from whom I inherited my love for writing and my talent.

To my brothers, Stu and Randy Carter, who share my love for baseball in general, and the Mets in particular and with whom I still talk baseball and share opening day at Citi Field as well as memories of other games, including sitting in the upper deck for the second-ever game at Shea Stadium; and drinking from the 1962 Mets tumblers we got from our father buying Sunoco gas. And to the Huntington Public Library for its large collection of baseball books that helped fuel all our knowledge and appreciation of the sport.

Over a 34-year stretch at Newsday, there are many people who were positive influences on my journalistic career. I would like to single out three: Howard Schneider, the then-managing editor who asked a news guy to take a spin at sports journalism; Harvey Aronson, who loved to talk writing at the drop of a hat; and Rich Galant, who let me write a column with a voice unlike any other at the paper.

In his acknowledgments, Mark has listed all of the people who assisted in the production of this book: the former players, the celebrities, the enablers. No need to list them again; I second Mark in expressing appreciation, although I would be remiss if I did not single out Ken Samelson, who provided the needed backstopping as the book's editor.

Finally, my deepest appreciation to Mark Rosenman for letting me share so many experiences over the years as your assistant coach and SportsTalkNY sidekick, for the wackiness that followed us from Disney to Cooperstown to Baseball Heaven to the makeshift broadcast studio in your spare bedroom, to the 540AM WLIE studios to asking me to write Glove Story with you. To borrow a classic line from Yogi Berra: Thank you for making this all necessary.

# PROLOGUE

We all make sacrifices for our children. We do this because we want them to achieve what we could not achieve. We want them to have what we could not have and to do what we could not do, and we long to live vicariously through them.

At the same time, we want our children to value what we value, not just embracing the moral compass that forms the fabric of our lives but sharing our likes and dislikes.

We work hard to forge bonds with our children, to bring them close and keep them close, even as they mature, move out and establish their own, independent lives. We create moments that become memories, and as we approach this stage of the life cycle, we struggle to find one last experience, one last memory, that will cement the parent-child bond before the inevitable break. We desperately try to cling to the essence of our relationship with our children even as we know we must both move on. But deep down, both parent and child know that no matter how much time and distance pass, no matter how melancholy they feel knowing their lives are about to diverge even further, they will always be able to draw on their common experience base to bring themselves closer again.

Many things can become the catalyst for these relationships —the love of music, or reading, or the outdoors, or cars, or fixing things, to name a few.

And then there's baseball.

More than any other sport, baseball helps create the lifelong memories and bonds. Start with something as simple as having a catch, which forges a one-on-one relationship practically from infancy, graduates to the backyard and finally to a playing field. How significant is the bond formed by a father and son having a catch? Think of the powerful scene in the film "*Field of Dreams*" in which Ray Kinsella, the main character, meets the younger version of his father, John. What do they do after the basic introductions? They have a catch, which makes the statement about what brings the generations together.

The next rite of passage is the son's first real baseball glove and the ritual in which the father painstakingly imparts the step-by-step process of breaking in the glove: what oil to use, where to place the oil, how to work the oil into the leather, and finally, how to create a pocket by finding the exact spot to place a baseball before tying the glove and leaving it sit so the oil can do its work. More than a secret handshake, this process represents the next step toward admission in the father-child club.

From having a catch, to learning how to throw and hit, father and child (traditionally son, but not just son any longer) progress to watching games together, first on television and later in person at ballfields and stadiums. In terms of relationships, what makes baseball unique among all the other sports is the relaxed pace, which allows for intense back and forth between the generations: questions asked and answered, stories told and retold, all the time cementing the link between the parent and the child and creating unforgettable moments.

We all remember the first time our father took us to a baseball game -who was playing, where we sat, who won, what were the highlights. And maybe we remember what our father told us during the game to pass from generation to generation the lore that makes baseball a sport beloved like no other. Something about a player we idolized? Something about the ballpark itself? Or, maybe, something about the first game he went to with his father?

When the child becomes old enough for Little League, and the father signs on to be a coach, their relationship enters a different phase. The instruction becomes more intense, as do the demands from both sides. And, perhaps, the child starts molding into a carbon copy of the father, following in the father's footsteps and - at least in the hopes and dreams of the father - beyond. Travel baseball morphs into playing for the high school team, which morphs into playing in college, which morphs into finding a career in the baseball industry for the son that the father nurtured in his dreams but did not or could not pursue.

This chronology could define many fathers and sons, but if certainly defines the relationship between Mark Rosenman and his son, Josh. Ask anybody who knew them during Josh's childhood, and the common conclusion was that Josh was Mark's son, no doubt about it. They shared the same interests. Mark imparted to Josh his love of movies, dogs, comedy, music, the New York Mets and the New York Rangers and his dislike of the New York Islanders. But most importantly, Mark and Josh forged their close relationship over baseball.

Mark coached Josh through Little League and travel baseball. He formed a travel team, ostensibly to keep his son and his son's friends together through high school, but at least from the perspective from a step away as Mark's assistant coach, to maintain the relationship with his son. There were ups and downs, successes and failures, as Josh made the high school baseball team, considered college ball only to quit when he realized his future lay not on a baseball field but in a discipline that required concentrating on his studies. Through an internship, he found a baseball job that showcased his artistic talents, allowing Mark (using the Yiddish phrases) to kvell and shep nachas.

Mark, meanwhile, found an outlet to satisfy his sportswriter and baseball player niche, covering the New York Mets as part of his weekly sports talk radio show gig, while discovering the subculture of frustrated, wannabe baseball players who scratch their competitive itch by attending a baseball fantasy camp. They mingle for a week with some of their favorite former players, get treated as if they were major leaguers, and generally try to turn back the clock to fantasize about what might have been.

Mark covered some fantasy camps as a reporter, and then played in two more. And as Josh made two of the more forceful statements about adulthood, becoming engaged and buying an apartment, Mark came up with the idea for one last father-son bonding memory: why don't they both go to fantasy camp together? And if they went, what would each of them have to do to keep from embarrassing themselves to each other, and to the camp at large?

For them, this would provide an even more specialized niche in the fantasy baseball camp realm: living the dream about not just what it would be a major leaguer, but experience the thrill of becoming part of the exclusive club of fathers and sons who have played together on a major league field - the Griffeys (Ken Sr. and Jr.), the Raineses (Tim Sr. and Jr.) and the Duncans (Frank Jr. and III, whose time together with the 1941 Negro League Kansas City Monarchs may have been the first).

That's what this book is all about: A last-fling tale that each of us would like to have with our children, rooted in the common thread that has helped define our lives. It is a tale that will bare their memories, hopes and dreams, in their words and from a step removed. It is a tale with humor and pathos (or is bathos?), and inspiration and a lot of perspiration, a story we all have lived or would like to live.

This is Mark and Josh Rosenman's story. But it just as easily could be yours.

.

# CHAPTER 1
## IN THE BEGINNING (BIG INNING)

On December 1, 1988, Josh Rosenman was born at North Shore University Hospital in Manhasset, Long Island, to Mark and Beth Rosenman. Thanks to a sonogram, Mark and Beth knew that their first child would be a boy, although that fact bore no special significance to Mark.

"I guess as a father, you always want a boy, but my thought was that we got it out of the way," Mark recalled, noting that he and Beth wanted two children, one boy and one girl. "But, really, it was whatever it was, like the old Jewish tradition, as long as it's healthy, it's got 10 fingers, 10 toes, I'm happy, so I was happy."

Under Jewish tradition, or maybe Jewish superstition, one does not prepare a baby's room until after he or she is born, so there was no sports-themed nursery waiting for Josh when Beth and Mark took Josh home to their house on Barbera Road in

Commack. But once home, it was clear that Josh's nursery would take on a sports theme. That included his crib bumpers, the mobile over the crib, the decorations on the walls. But they were, for want of a better description, sports eclectic-the mobile, for example, was football-reflecting Mark's overall passion for everything sports related. The focus on baseball would come later, a choice more the son's than the father's.

Mark does not remember his first catch with Josh. Unlike many other fathers, he did not buy a glove for Josh even before his son would come home from the hospital, and he did not have any grand master plan to introduce his son to any of the sports that contributed to his sports passion-in particular, baseball and hockey. He would eventually purchase a toddler baseball set for Josh-manufactured by Fisher Price, the toy company, not a sports equipment brand. Most likely, the set included a plastic bat and ball and a batting tee.

Josh's first tee work. (Photo courtesy of Mark Rosenman)

"He would go out on the lawn, and he would hit the ball," Mark remembered. "He was a big kid, and he would hit the ball pretty far. I think at that point, we probably got a ball and just would have a catch. It was probably like me throwing to him, and him just sticking his hand out, and the ball going over his glove or under his glove, and then me trying to toss the ball so it would hit his glove." The glove was plastic, and the ball may have been, too, or even a tennis ball.

As Josh tells it, Mark was not the most patient of fathers as trying to master catching a thrown ball, and Mark's actions were no harbinger of the important role baseball would play in their relationship. "My earliest memory was him being really aggravated that I would never be able to hit him in the chest and he'd have to keep running after balls," Josh remembered. "It got to a point where I could never get it to him, so he got me one of those pitchbacks."  That way, Josh could learn to catch and throw without needing a foil, or a frustrated father, to chase bad throws or try to aim the ball into a glove.

Like Mark, Josh does not remember his first glove, but he does remember his first bat, a style called "Connections," a two-piece bat with a rubber piece separating barrel from grip. The brand was Easton, and Josh remembers the big red lettering on the barrel.

Josh also does not remember any conscious effort on his father's part to channel his interests toward baseball. He didn't have to. All Josh needed to do was wander into the spare bedroom in their house, a four-bedroom contemporary in an upscale neighborhood in a middle-class Long Island community. There, Mark and Beth had assembled a shrine to their separate collectible passions: cookie jars for Beth and baseball memorabilia for Mark.

Signed baseballs-Josh particularly remembers ones inked by Mickey Mantle and Whitey Ford; complete Topps baseball card sets for every year from 1966; yearbooks; commemorative Coke bottles (there also was an old Coke vending machine, with the hand crank to select a bottle). And Mark-specific memorabilia: Mark, in his college days (with hair, Josh noted) interviewing major-league baseball players for his college radio station.

Mark with hair and Hall of Famer Willie Stargell. (Photo courtesy of Mark Rosenman)

"You walked into that room and you could see he was seriously obsessed with baseball," Josh noted. "It was a pretty cool room. It had a lot of cool stuff. I touched everything, and I would always bring friends."

Josh's sister, Liana, would come along 18 months after he was born, and while both parents doted on each of their children, as Josh and Liana advanced in their formative years, it would become very noticeable to Mark and Beth's friends that from a personality standpoint, Josh was very much Mark's child and Liana, Beth's. Josh would embrace Mark's love of music (which would result in piano lessons that uncovered musical talent), crass humor, hockey (the New York Rangers in particular) and baseball (the New York Mets, but more about that in a later chapter).

"Josh was a very social kid. He always loved being around people doing things," Mark said. "He would love watching music videos on television. I don't know if he took to baseball more than some of the other things. He always enjoyed everything."

Mark never realized the role baseball was playing above the other interests as Josh grew up.

"I knew early on that I definitely wanted to play baseball," Josh said. "Just watching, it was always exciting. Even as a kid, I never really got distracted. I was always paying attention to the game."

Josh's career in organized baseball got off to an auspicious start, one that would take him and Mark on a 13-year journey that Mark had never envisioned; one in which baseball would bring them close and keep them close.

For some fathers, coaching their son in Little League baseball, or in any youth sport for that matter, is part of a well-crafted, long-designed plan that probably has a tantalizing unachievable goal of ensuring a college scholarship or professional athletic career. Those fathers believe they, and they alone, should control their child's sports destiny, and they view the remaining members of their teams as mere supporting players to help advance their child's progress. More often than not, this control-freak tendency drives an irreparable wedge between father and son rather than producing and continuing closeness.

Others know at the moment of their child's birth that they will become his or her coach because they want to make the statement to their children that they are "regular guys," that their dad is cool enough for them and their friends to hang out with.

Some remember their fathers as their coach, and the warm feeling they got from seeing their father lead them, and their friends, to victory. They volunteer as coaches to establish and cement with their child the same bond their father maintained with them.

And then there are fathers who stumble into coaching by accident. Like Mark.

Mark had no intention of becoming Josh's T-ball coach when he signed him up in a league based not in their community, Commack, Long Island, but in the neighboring one of Kings Park. Both communities have baseball histories that include major leaguers: Pete Harnisch, who pitched for the Cincinnati Reds and the New York Mets, hailed from Commack, and Kings Park is best known from a baseball perspective as the hometown, of Hall of Famer Craig Biggio. (Mark would attribute Kings Park equal sports stature as the home of NHL enforcer and New York Ranger Jim Pavese.)

At the time, the Commack North Little League did not offer T-ball, but Kings Park did, and Mark did not want Josh, a big kid for his age, to wait a year to play ball. So Kings Park it was, and Mark signed Josh up to add T-ball to an already hectic schedule of soccer, Cub Scouts, and piano lessons. Somewhat incongruously, the league was run by the local Catholic church, making Josh more than geographically out of place.

Craig Biggio's Hall of Fame career started in Kings Park. (Photo courtesy of eschipul on Flickr [CC BY-SA 2.0 (https://creativecommons.org/licenses/by-sa/2.0)]))

Excitedly, Mark brought Josh to the first practice, to meet his coach. Mark immediately knew there was a problem. "I kind of got a weird vibe because he was struggling, looking for the equipment in the car, and something seemed off. When he introduced himself to the parents, I realized what it was."

So did the other parents: The coach, showing up for his first practice coaching five-year-old-T-ball, at 7 o'clock on a Saturday morning, reeked of alcohol.

While Morris Buttermaker may have been acceptable as coach of the Bad News Bears, what flies in fictional Southern California does not in more uptight and proper real-life Kings Park, New York. Parents, Mark included, complained.

"I called up and said, listen, I want him on another team, and they said, all the teams are set, we'll have to find another parent to coach. I said, 'I'll do it, it's not a big deal, it's T-ball. Little did I know at the time that this would become a 13-year labor of love that would take us through 1,000 games, tournaments up and down the East Coast, and a lot of memorable moments in-between."

At this point, it is worth pausing in the narrative of Josh's developmental years to look at Mark's.

For the most part, we want our children's childhoods to mirror ours, for them to participate in the same activities, play the same games, and experience the same simple pleasures. That way, we can develop common interests and share the joys that are part of growing up. The challenge is that changing times often make replicating the fundamentals of our childhoods difficult, if not impossible, but we try nevertheless.

What Mark wanted for Josh was his typical suburban childhood, one rooted not in over-organized scheduled activities supervised by parents or parent surrogates, but in spontaneous play arranged by neighborhood contemporaries. Seaford, Long Island, where Mark grew up in the 1960s, was a typical suburban community, populated by New York City emigres who all were in the same life stage when they moved into their new houses to raise families of children who were all about the same age. There was no shortage of boys with whom he could play without having to arrange a play date and no shortage of back and front yards, as well as the street, that they could use as playing fields.The neighborhood also had no shortage of raconteurs-all of the fathers, it seemed, had large repertoires of stories to tell the younger generation. Some stories had their roots in their own childhoods, others in their experiences during World War II or the Korean War.

And then there were those with sports yarns to spin, including a neighbor, Max Wolsky, who eagerly regaled the neighborhood youth with tales of his time as a hurler in the St. Louis Browns' minor league system, along with pitching tips. Mark's father, Morris, offered advice on football technique, citing as his bona fides playing on the undefeated Seward Park High School gridiron champions, with a wistful note about how the War prevented him from accepting an offer to play for the Chicago Bears.

Morris Rosenman (#78 ) and his 1939 Seward Park High team. (Photo courtesy of Mark Rosenman)

Unlike today, when children at a very young age are channeled into becoming specialists in a single sport, which runs year-round, Mark's choice of playtime sports activities varied from season to season. During football season he along with the Petrizzos, (Anthony and Tommy), Stuart Sloan, Paul Somin, and Jeff Cohen played a variant they called offense-defense, in which one person was the official quarterback and the others alternated being on offense and defense. During basketball season, he would play in front of his house, using the basket his father had put up.

When he was old enough to experience his first taste of organized sports, well, that was really special, largely because it was so different than the playtime pickup games and unlike any of his other activities. The Mayfair Little League was set up to mimic professional baseball, with different levels called Single A, Double A, Triple A , and the Majors. They played on two different fields, Seamans Neck School and Washington Park, which had perfectly manicured diamonds that made them feel like professional ballplayers. The fields were equidistant from the neighborhood 7-Eleven and the all-important postgame Slurpee.

Mark's Little League career spanned several  years, and hit its stride when, playing at the Triple-A level at the age of 11, he made the All-Star Game and followed that up the next year by playing in the Majors on a championship team.

Mark never played travel baseball-such as it was at the time -and at no time during his Little League career was Morris Rosenman  his coach. "My father came to all of my games," Mark said, "but I had different coaches throughout all of my Little League. I have really good memories of all those coaches."

One, in particular, stood out. His name was Frank Santoriello, and he coached Mark and his friends to a championship. Back then, Mark never knew the details of Coach Santoriello's life, only that he seemed dedicated to the players and taught them the fundamentals of the game and the need to focus on playing well.

Coach Santoriello and the 1972 Champs. (Photo courtesy of Ken Ricken)

Decades later, Mark would learn the full story, partly in a reconnecting phone call with his coach, but largely through an email from the coach's son and Mark's teammate, Frank Jr.

Coach Santoriello, it turned out, was a decorated World War II and Korean War veteran whose war souvenirs included metal plates in both legs and multiple skin grafts after being hit with shrapnel and that he was only able to walk by undergoing years of physical therapy. As Frank Jr. would note, sometimes while running up and down the sidelines coaching (he coached baseball, football and lacrosse), the skin grafts would start to bleed. So as a prophylactic, he would wrap his legs in bandages so his children and his charges could not see.

Frank Jr. was one of nine children, all adopted, and his father was dedicated to all of them. While he was busy as an accountant, he made sure to find time to coach, even during busy season. And there was no ulterior, long-term motive, he noted recently. "It kept them out of trouble," he said. "That was the most important thing to me, anyway."

And his actions did inspire his oldest son, Frank. Jr. "I don't have a son, but I have two daughters and I coached their softball teams and then coach their soccer teams," Frank Jr. said. "And it's because my dad found the time to coach us that I made sure I made the time to coach them."

That example, and that model, also rubbed off on Mark.

1972 Giants reunion, Frank Jr. , Frank and Mark. (Photo courtesy of Mark Rosenman)

Fast forward back to the T-ball field, with Mark suddenly taking on the coach's mantle and Josh among the eager learners. "I enjoyed teaching the kids, showing them how to hold the bat and throw the ball to the bases," Mark said. "So I figured, it was fun, let me keep doing it. So when we moved over to Commack North the next year, I signed up to coach."

In Josh, at least, he had an eager pupil. "I knew early on that I wanted to play baseball," Josh said. "Just watching it, it was always exciting. Even as a kid, I never got distracted. I was always paying attention to the game and I would always be thinking ahead, like, oh, why aren't they doing this? Why aren't they doing that?"

Baseball was one of the vehicles-music was a second - through which Josh channeled his drive to be the best at whatever he did. "I always had a big self-drive to get better, to do things better. When it came to the things I enjoy doing, I wanted to be one of the better ones doing it."

His father's role? "He pushed me. He expected a lot out of me. He probably expected more than I expected out of myself. But baseball and homelife were two pretty different things. It never carried over at the end of the game, except when I did something good. If I did something good. I would gloat about it for a while, and he would tell my mom she should have been at the game. But even younger, I remember, every home run I hit, he made sure somebody got it. He would write the date on it, and he would write the opposing pitcher on it, a Little League pitcher, just in case, I guess, somewhere down the line, if the pitcher became someone, he could say I hit a home run off him way back when. It seems a little excessive, but I had those balls for a long time."

Josh's earliest home run balls- complete with date and opposing pitcher. (Photo courtesy of Mark Rosenman)

"I probably was a little too tough on him and pushed him," Mark admitted. "But, you know, he also set his goals. He wanted to make the high school team. So as a parent, you tell your kid, if you want to be an accountant, you need to ace your math. If you want to be a musician, you have to learn things other than just the music you like.

"His goal was that he wanted to make the high school team, so when he didn't make the junior high school team, he was devastated. There were people who felt he wasn't given a shot, even looked at. Some of that might have had to do with his physical size at that point. He really hadn't grown into his body by any means. He hadn't gone through a growth spurt. So I would tell him you need to run a little bit, you need to do this. If I had to do it all over again, I don't know if I would have done that."

But Mark is unapologetic about the times he did get angry at Josh. "I never, ever got mad at Josh for physical errors, or for striking out. The things that really irritated me were the mental errors because I felt that was just a lack of a concentration. I always thought he was better than that. So those were the areas where I don't think I ever cut him slack."

But we're getting ahead of ourselves again. Mark coached Josh through the regular Little League season and then on a travel team that, while not the Bad News Bears, nevertheless played with a chip on its shoulder, beginning as the Commack North Little League's "B" travel squad the Cougars,with something very much to prove. And in Mark, they had a coach who instilled in his team a sense that they would overcome talent limitations through perseverance and passion. "I'm sure from the outside looking in, from the amount of times I got thrown out of games, probably people looked at me like, this guy's crazy," Mark said .(Authors' note: we can hear all those heads nodding.) But that demeanor helped foster an us-against-the-world attitude that pushed the team to reach, and exceed, its potential. Even if that meant playing at a level well beyond its abilities.

Mark used various incentives to goad his team into success. One was a promise that if they reached certain milestones-with a point system set up for each-he would sign the team up for a tournament at Disney World in Orlando, Florida. "It was a team-based goal, focused on the basics of backing up position, hustling to and from the dugout between innings, and keeping helmets and bats orderly in the dugout," Mark remembered. "It kept the kids focused, for sure, which was important for kids that age, who tend to daydream or fool around. We still allowed fun and kid stuff, but we were there for baseball."

Mark would counterbalance the serious-in-the-dugout posture by scheduling off-the-field nights designed for team bonding, at backyard pools and video game arcades. In doing that,

Mark keep the team close and kept himself close to the lives of Josh and his friends.

In the off-seasons, Mark kept the team together by scheduling indoor instructional clinics with professional coaches (some with major-league experience) and by entering the team in an indoor winter baseball league at a facility in Hauppauge, Long Island, called Play Ball.

Play Ball was better in concept than in practice. Its operators imposed some unusual ground rules, based on its physical limitations (think about the rules peculiar to the Tampa Bay Rays' Tropicana Field and you get the general idea), and the building had lighting, ventilation and drainage issues that produced a mustiness that made spectators (especially parents) uncomfortable, if not alarmed. For the players, however, especially those as young as the Cougars, and those not used to turf fields and excited about mimicking major leaguers than playing at Houston's Astrodome and Seattle's Kingdome, Play Ball provided the ultimate winter baseball experience.

Play Ball the ultimate winter experience. (Photo courtesy of Mark Rosenman)

The team competed against squads from other Long Island communities, and while the Cougars were not necessarily, or demonstrably, the best team in their league, they at least were competitive. And in staying together in winter, and playing baseball, the Cougars continued to rack up points, bringing them closer to going to Disney World.

It took the team two years to accumulate the requisite 100 points, from the time they were 10 until the time they were just short of 12. And for Memorial Day Weekend 2001, Mark entered them in a tournament with, essentially, a national representation of teams, all with more high-level competition experience than Mark's Commack Cougars. Not to mention a set of rules unfamiliar to 11-year-olds trained in Little League.

Instead of 60-foot basepaths and no leading or stealing until the ball had passed home plate (rules common to Williamsport, Pennsylvania-based Little League), they would be playing with bases 75 feet apart and major league-style leading and stealing. Mark and his assistant coaches tried, best they could, to school the team in these new rules-while playing under the old ones during their Little League season. Primary leads, secondary leads, holding runners on, balk-free pickoff moves. Not to mention the extra energy for running from one base to another and the additional distance to throw to a base. And add the complication of not being able to play-or coach-a single game using those rules.

It could have been the recipe for disaster, and on one level - the competitive one-it was. But on the more important level-the one that fostered teamwork and created a bonding experience for teammates and their parents,-it was an unmitigated success.

The trip had an auspicious beginning, with flight problems that nearly scuttled the trip. The team's flight, from Long Island

MacArthur Airport in Islip, was first delayed and then canceled - with the airline saying the next flight with available space was on Memorial Day, after the tournament would be over. Mustering his controlled anger and threatening the airline with a media story of a youth baseball team stranded and unable to go to Disney World (with the accompanying visual of 11-year-olds, in uniform around an airport baggage carousel with forlorn looks on their faces).,Mark cajoled the airline into finding them space on a jumbo jet about to leave a few hours later-from Newark Liberty Airport, 75 miles away.

The team, parents, and siblings piled onto a bus provided by the airline and began the trip to New Jersey. Until they encountered a major traffic jam. Unless traffic suddenly cleared up, which was unlikely, they would again be shut out of a flight taking them to Disney.

Drawing on what was then a novel device-his cell phone - Mark established contact with the airline's regional manager, and with the threat of an unfavorable media story continuing to loom, Mark remained in contact with the manager, who held the plane until the team got there. Immediately after boarding the jumbo jet, the gates closed.

The Cougars arrived at the Disney Wide World of Sports complex shortly after midnight and were not able to check into their rooms until about an hour or two later-some into rooms that did not have working air conditioning. A coaches meeting was scheduled for 9 o'clock that morning and the first game a few hours after that. Even under the best of circumstances, the games were going to be a challenge, with the stiffer competition and he unfamiliar rules. Factor in the exhaustion from the trip, and it was a recipe for disaster. Which, from a competition perspective, it was. Not a single win, and no games that could be considered even close. Playing largely against teams from warmer-weather climates experienced in the more challenging competition, the Cougars were more than outclassed. They were annihilated.

The on-field highlight-especially for Josh-indelibly etched into the memories of Cougar players and parents alike, was Mark getting thrown out of one of the games for arguing with an umpire.

"I vaguely remember it was our first game," Mark said, "early in the morning. Our kids were dragging. They were tired, it was very hot, and we were playing a team that may have been from the Dominican Republic. Or so it seemed. They were bigger than us, and they spoke a language other than English.

"One of our players, Matt Baren, walked, and was bunted over to second. The pitcher threw a ball into the dirt, and Matt took off for third. He slid in, spikes unintentionally a little high, and was tagged out. The third baseman took exception to that and shoved Matt. I yelled at the umpires that they shouldn't allow the shove. There was a no-tolerance rule for yelling at umpires, so he threw me out. I explained in a nice way that there also was a no tolerance rule for players and the shove was not acceptable, but it didn't matter."

Memories may be a bit hazy, or at least Mark's memory. A photograph capturing the moment-one Mark notes "shows up on Facebook every now and then"-depicts Mark considerably more animated, and considerably less in control, than he remembers. But ask Josh about his favorite memory of the tournament, and maybe his favorite memory of Mark as coach, and his response comes quickly and decisively: "Getting thrown out at Disney."

Getting tossed at Disney. (Photo courtesy of A.J. Carter)

That actually says a lot, because over the years, Mark developed a large body of work being thrown out of games for arguing with umpires.

But again, we're getting ahead of ourselves.

In July, 1996, a man named Louis Presutti opened a youth baseball mecca on 156 acres about five miles south of Cooperstown, New York, the town where legend has it that Abner Doubleday invented baseball and where, as a result, the National Baseball Hall of Fame was established in 1939.

Presutti's father, also named Louis, had played semi-pro baseball and barnstormed with the Belmont Athletics on a circuit in Ohio, Pennsylvania, New Jersey, and New York from 1927 until the outbreak of World War II, right around the time Lou Jr. was born.

The senior Presutti passed on his love of baseball to his son, and then to his grandson Lou, both of whom would accompany him on trips to Cooperstown for fishing and pilgrimages to the Hall of Fame. On one of those outings, as the legend promulgated and repeated by the middle-generation Lou goes, his father looked around the historic village and exclaimed to son and grandson Lous: "Every kid in America should have the opportunity to play baseball in Cooperstown."

Thus was planted in Lou Jr.'s mind the idea of a baseball mecca dedicated not to the Babe Ruths, Ty Cobbs, Ken Griffey Jr.s, ,Mike Piazzas, Randy Johnsons, et al ,of the world, but to the 12-year-old aspiring star who dreamed of a major-league career and not just a league, but a hall of fame of his own.

So when patriarch Lou passed away in 1992, scion Lou set out to fulfill his father' s pronouncement and satisfy what had become a dream of his own, as he developed and continued an affiliation with youth baseball that spanned 34 years. "I needed purpose to build this," Lou Jr. would tell espn.com in 2013, a few years before his own passing. "I coached for 34 years, involved with youth baseball at the 12-year-old level, and I needed something else, too. My purpose really was that I love this game so much and love what it will lend you if you allow it to."

Lou. Jr., who had a successful career in target marketing, invested his savings into buying the land and building what he would name Cooperstown Dreams Park, which opened in 1996. He built fields,barracks to house teams, and facilities to feed the teams and well as the needs and desires of families who would follow their budding stars (and also feed the local economy by filling hotels and restaurants). He started with a four-week season and 30 teams a week; over the years that mushroomed to more than 100 teams a week for a 12-week season. Presutti created the American

Youth Baseball Hall of Fame, with its own record book and an ever-growing list of "records" tailored to the wide spectrum of competitors who spend a week at the park.

Among the eclectic list: most pickles by a player called safe in a week; most home runs and foul balls returned by a player; first girl to pitch for a win; first family to have three brothers each hit a home run; shortest and tallest players to hit a home run (51.75 inches and 76.5 inches, respectively). Want to create a record? Submit it to management for review.

Cooperstown Dreams Park developed a reputation for attracting the best players from around the country. Umpires flocked to the complex, volunteering their professional services in return only for room and board, for the opportunity to be able to say-if and when -"I umpired a game (fill in the blank) played when he was 12 years old." Children of major leaguers-including Roger Clemens, Greg Maddux and hockey legend Wayne Gretzky-would spend time at Dreams Park, as well as some who would grow up to be major leaguers themselves, such as Mike Trout, Chris Sale and David Price. When Lou Jr. passed away in 2016, Bryce Harper, another Dreams Park alumnus, then with the Washington Nationals posted on Facebook: "You will be missed, Lou! This man touched more lives and made more dreams come true than anybody that I know."

Fulfilling dreams, as well as proving the Cougars belonged in upper-level if not elite competition, was very much on Mark Rosenman's mind when he signed the team up for a week at Cooperstown Dreams Park in August 2001. Only five years after its creation, competing in Cooperstown had attracted a national roster of teams and, locally, among Long Island's Little League travel teams, become the entry fee into the conversation over the best local squads. For the Commack North Little League, it was naturally assumed that the "A" travel team would make the trip (they did, for a week in June that year) playing at Cooperstown, and acquitting itself respectably, would once again validate the B-team Cougars' consideration as a team with talent. Not to mention the team-bonding opportunity that Mark, as head coach, could share with his charges, Josh included, both as adult chaperone and as participant: no need to live vicariously through Josh the experience Mark wished had existed when he was Josh's age.

Unlike Disney, the Cougars were better prepared for this tournament, having competed in a Long Island summer travel league and won a championship-its first, and, it would prove, only, in its history. Mark also enlisted for the tournament a youth who played occasionally with the Cougars but who for the most part competed on a much higher level; Mike Belfiore would go on to a college baseball career, be drafted by the Arizona Diamondbacks, play several years in the minor leagues and appear briefly in a major-league game. Even at the age of 12, his seriousness and preparation went well beyond the merely talented player, and, as a bow to the need to preserve his pitching arm, he was sneaked out of the Cooperstown barracks each night and slept in more comfortable surroundings with his family in a motel.

The Cooperstown experience got off to a less auspicious start than Disney, with families driving individually to the complex. Once there, parents checked their sons in to the team's barracks, and then left them to the care of Mark, his two assistant coaches, and an additional parent who had signed on as a chaperone.

The Cougars in the barracks at Cooperstown Dreams Park. (Photo courtesy of A.J. Carter)

Mark's memories of the Dreams Park experience are vivid; not so Josh's. He remembered some of the scatological-based hijinks, meeting players from around the country and trading pins, a Dreams park tradition, and the team getting to carry out a promise Mark made to them as an incentive for winning: the opportunity to shave his head if they won a certain number of consecutive games. Which they did, thanks to one of (at least to Mark) of the more stunning victories: a come-from-behind win on a bottom of the last inning squeeze bunt against another Long Island squad, from the nearby community of Massapequa. That team gained some measure of fame by barely missing making the Little League World Series the month before, losing to a team from the Bronx that would become the darlings of New York city by finishing third in the competition before being disqualified after it was discovered some weeks later that their star pitcher, a youth named Danny Almonte, was two years over the age limit. Interestingly, the Cougars' win would come at about the same time that Almonte was pitching the Rolando Paulino All-Stars to the semi-finals; the games would be on the television back at the motel.

There are photographs of the Cougars celebrating after that win, and of them shaving Mark's head. To Mark, this was a major team-bonding moment. Not so, apparently to Josh. "He really was pretty much bald, so it wasn't that big of a deal," Josh said 17 years later. "It's not like they gave him a tattoo or something."

"It's not like they gave him a tattoo or something." (Photo courtesy of A.J. Carter)

But the Dreams Park tournament, unlike Disney, would prove that the Cougars had the talent to be middle of the pack. Overall, they went 4-5 that week, ranking 35th out of the 48 teams. The four wins and a one-run loss were against Long Island and New Jersey-based teams. The other four losses were blowouts from the western half of the United States, including one to a similarly-nicknamed California team. The California Cougars had demonstrated their seriousness of purpose by posting a sign on their barracks that they would not trade pins (and, essentially, that they would not fraternize with the other players) until the games were over. They would end up finishing third.

The Commack Cougars would make it into the Dreams Park record book for the shortest battery to pitch and catch. Alas, the record was fleeting: there is currently no mention of it on the Dreams Park website.

Mark remembers the team visit to the Hall of Fame, and the serendipity of encountering former New York Yankees third baseman Clete Boyer on a downtown street and engaging him in a conversation abruptly cut short when the ex-major leaguer decided that a tree on the street needed trimming and went to his van to get pruning shears. They would try to continue the conversation the next day by dining at Boyer's restaurant, Clete Boyer's Hamburger Hall of Fame, but, alas, Boyer wasn't there. He probably was out trimming trees.

Evan Carter's chance encounter with former Yankee Clete Boyer (Photo courtesy of A.J. Carter)

Mark was excited to be showing Josh and the entire team baseball's most famous shrine, and photographs depict the team cavorting in Hank Aaron's locker and starting at the plaques of baseball's immortals. It was Josh's first and so far only time at the Hall of Fame. "I wasn't blown away by it," he said, recalling with greater fondness the visit to the shop that produced a bat with his name on it and the time spent at the go-kart track.

Which brings us back to Lou Presutti Jr., Dreams Park's founder, who would comment on his vision in the 2013 espn.com interview: "We have a thing here at Cooperstown Dreams Park. The most important thing is to be your own hero and you need to dream dreams. And you've got to be willing to pay the price to make those dreams come true. And when they don't come true, you have to instantly begin to dream new dreams."

The Cougars at the end of a memorable week in Cooperstown. (Photo courtesy of Mark Rosenman)

As they drove home from Dreams Park, Mark was already dreaming.

\*\*\*

For most children, organized baseball ends at 12, the age limit for participation in Little League. Having dabbled at hardball and having discovered their talents lay elsewhere, they direct their attention to other sports or other pursuits: drama, music, service clubs at school, more intensive studies, bar or bat mitzvah lessons. Dreams of major league careers, or at least college scholarships, have long since been stifled by the harsh reality that they lack the ability, or, perhaps, the dedication and drive to succeed at any level higher than recreation league baseball or softball. The decision to end pursuing a baseball player's life can also be fueled by a parent's lack of commitment, in time and in dollars, required from them for their child to compete on a higher level.

For others, the dream remains alive-whether it be to play varsity high school baseball, earn a college athletic scholarship or a chance to play professional baseball. If they didn't already know it at 12, they would soon learn that the path gets exponentially more difficult as they try to climb the next rung on the ladder. They continue playing, as long as some ember from the baseball player fire burns within.

Josh's goal was on the modest end of the scale: to make his high school baseball team, following in his father's footsteps. Mark was happy to oblige by fulfilling his parental obligation to secure professional instruction for Josh (batting and, mostly, pitching lessons by former professional ballplayers, including some former major leaguers).

Without going into details, let's just say that Josh's physique was closer to Mickey Lolich than to Mickey Mantle, which placed him at a serious disadvantage in the eyes of a coach looking for easy reasons to whittle down a large tryout group to a playing roster.

Mark tried to use various motivational tools on Josh, including suggesting a rigorous running program to shape his body into a more athletic appearance-"if I had to do it over again, maybe I wouldn't have done that," he admitted – and made sure that Josh continued playing organized baseball by keeping the Commack Cougars alive and playing baseball.

"I don't know if it was a conscious decision," Mark said." I think because each year, we were getting more and more kids. There wasn't a lot of atrophy. We weren't losing kids, so it was clear they still wanted to be part of it. I was in for the ride, especially to see them grow from eight-year-old boys through high school. Watching just the difference in them and then becoming men was a pretty neat thing to see."

Not to mention the opportunity to deepen the bond between father and son.

"Because we spent so much time together, I knew a lot about him," Mark said of Josh. "There was a lot of togetherness, a lot of time. I don't know if anything else would have afforded that."

They would talk in the car about what Josh had learned during one of his lessons; about what Josh had done right or wrong during a game; about their mutual interest in music and their differing music tastes; about Josh's music talent and artistic ability; about cars and girls and Mark's other favorite sport, hockey, and Josh's career aspirations.

They talked, and Josh listened and learned. He began to understand his father's coaching methods (and would use them when he began coaching a a few years later), and the life lessons that underpinned them. "The big thing was accountability," Josh recalled. "You didn't show up for practice, you came late to a game, he didn't care if you were the best player, you're getting benched. And it was important that that the kids knew their roles."

As Josh matured through his teens, the Cougars,roster would change. Some of the originals, even though who had shared the Disney and Cooperstown experiences, would decide to spend time at pursuits other than baseball. Mark worked hard to find replacements on bulletin boards and through word of mouth. The replacements were, in many cases, more talented that the original Cougars, and more committed; a reflection of the natural winnowing process. They also had different personal agendas-something Josh noticed for himself year later when he coached a high-school-age team.

\*\*\*\*

Running what was essentially a freelance travel team for teenaged ballplayers, Mark would soon learn, entailed a lot more than scheduling practices and setting lineups for games. He was coach, general manager, business manager, treasurer and chief groundskeeper. Mark signed the Cougars up for a league, the National Junior Baseball League, that itself was essentially a one-man operation providing a schedule structure but little else.

Among Mark's responsibilities was ensuring that all of the players on his roster were current in paying their required fee so he had enough cash on hand to pay the umpires-a team, not a league responsibility in the NJBL. He also had to provide a field for the home games. Mark secured a permit to make a local middle school field the Cougars' home venue. The permit allowed the team to use the field-and provided written proof should someone else show up trying to use it-but no additional facilities and no day-of-game field preparation from school district employees. Not even when it rained.

This was significant because this particular field had drainage issues, not to mention a rutted infield that produced large puddles on the basepaths, particularly between second and third base. On those occasions, it was up to head groundskeeper Mark to bring out the rakes and bags of Diamond Dry, a chemical of undetermined composition that, if by magic, absorbs water and causes puddles to disappear.

The problem was, the Cougars needed to bring their own rakes and their own rakers-parents who had driven their sons to the game and had expected to merely become spectators, only to discover that the gardening chores they hoped to shirk by watching baseball had followed them to the ball field.

Coach and head groundskeeper Mark Rosenman. (Photo courtesy of Mark Rosenman)

Which brings us to what was essentially the straw that instead of drying the field broke the back of the Cougars' life span in the National Junior Baseball League. The Cougars' roster at that point consisted primarily, if not entirely, of players from the north end of Commack,who moved steadily through one little league. The opponents in this particular game were a team composed of players from the south end of the community, which had its own little league. The players were now attending a common middle school-the site of the Cougars' home field-and would compete for slots on the middle school baseball team. This was as close to a classic rivalry game as the Cougars would experience at this point in their history.

For weeks, Mark and the team had circled this game on their schedule. Excitement was high. Trash had been talked in the halls of Commack Middle School.

And then, the night before the game, it rained. Not quite a biblical rain, but close. When Mark, his assistant coaches, and the other parents arrived at the field, they found large puddles on the base paths, one so large that calling for a lifeguard seemed more appropriate than calling for Diamond Dry. They whipped out all the bags they had of the miracle powder. The tried rakes to move the water around. Then even brought a shop vac to the field, with about 300 feet of extension cord that, thanks to the one helpful act by a school employee, they were allowed to plug into a school outlet, probably in violation of their permit.

With faint fears of the mud between second and third turning into a sinkhole, the game began. Calling the field playable was a stretch; given the rivalry and the expectation, everybody wanted to stretch.

But not everybody was satisfied. One of the parents on the Commack South-based team was a local garbage carter and as the game began, he reached for his cell phone and began barking orders.

The Commack Middle School property was on a somewhat busy road, with the parking lot in front and the school in back. The field was set back by the gymnasium entrance to the school, about 700 to 800 feet from the road.

The players slogged through the top and bottom of the first inning, but as the second inning was about to start, a dump truck could be seen in the distance on the road. It turned into the parking lot and veered onto the outfield. The umpire stopped the game and joined the players in watching the spectacle of the approaching vehicle. As the truck got closer, it was easily identifiable as belonging to the carting company owned by the Commack South father.

The truck pulled up to the infield. Then turned around as it got to the fringe where a shortstop would normally stand. The back of the truck began lifting up; the back opened and suddenly a large load of dry dirt was deposited onto the infield. And just as quickly, the driver lowered the back down and drove away.

"Damnedest thing I have ever seen," the umpire commented as the parents picked up their cue, and their rakes, to spread the dirt around and eliminate any trace of puddle or suspected quicksand.

Mark got the message. For the next season, he entered the team in a league that played on artificial turf fields.

   \*\*\*

Not many people know of the Long Island community of Yaphank, but those who do appreciate its unusual history. During World War I, it was home to an Army base, Camp Upton, where Irving Berlin, who was stationed there, wrote "God Bless America" for a musical revue called "*Yip, Yip, Yaphank.*" Berlin pulled the song from the revue as being "too sticky," but did include the ditty, "Oh, How I Hate to Get Up in the Morning," which would become fleetingly popular. God Bless America would resurface during the runup to World War II in a revised, and more lasting, version.

Berlin composed *God Bless America* in Yaphank, N.Y.(Photo courtesy of Life magazine images [Public domain])

Shortly before World War II, a proposal was filed with the town clerk in Brookhaven, of which Yaphank is a part, to build a community called German Gardens, with streets named after Adolf Hitler and his henchmen, Joseph Goebbels and Herman Goering.

The site, at the time also known as Camp Siegfried, became the headquarters for the Nazi-leaning German American Bund and the location of pro-Nazi rallies. The street names were changed after the US entered the war and government prosecutions stopped the rallies, but legend has it that after a German submarine was intercepted off the Hamptons community of Amagansett, German spies arrested on shore had tickets to the Yaphank movie theater in their pocket.

Training day at Camp Siegfried prior to World War II.(Photo courtesy of FBI [Public domain])

In the 1980s, after an explosion at their fireworks factory in Bellport killed two family members and damaged 100 nearby houses, the internationally-acclaimed Grucci family moved their operations to Yaphank after executing a land swap with Suffolk County, trading 131 acres of pine barrens forestland that was the largest remaining supply of pure groundwater in the county for an

88-acre plot suitably isolated from other buildings to be safely separated should another unfortunate explosion or fire occur.

Not quite the bucolic, historic, baseball-rich community that is Cooperstown, but to an entrepreneur named Andy Borgia, it was heaven. Baseball Heaven, to be specific, a complex he built in the hopes that teams would come. Borgia arranged for $8.5 million in financing, cleared a 28-acre tract nowhere near the Gruccis and erected a state-of-the-art complex with four major-league-size fields and three 75-foot diamonds for those looking to ease from Little League to full size (the same length as the basepaths the Cougars played years before in the Disney tournament). "My dream was to build a place where kids could play in a healthy, safe environment and learn the game," Borgia said in a 2004 newspaper interview, around the time the complex opened. "Baseball Heaven is here to take the dream of playing like a professional player and make it a reality."

Borgia's vision was that he would fill the fields with tournament teams from the Northeast, if not the entire country, hoping that the high quality of the facilities would attract top-quality talent, who would be observed by college and major-league scouts watching the games.

The fields had below-grade professional dugouts and full-length bullpens, electric scoreboards, stadium seating and announcers' towers. Batting cages with pitching machines were near the fields. And, oh yes, artificial turf.

That was the feature that caused Mark Rosenman to take notice. This was his own version of baseball heaven: fields that if it rained, would be somebody else's responsibility to make playable, and with artificial turf, the probability that field condition would not be a factor in deciding if a game was to go on. He began inquiring about the league play that would keep the fields active during off-tournament months and quickly-months before Baseball Heaven was completed-signed up the Cougars for one of the initial leagues. So excited was Mark that he would frequently make the half-hour drive from his house to check on the construction progress.

Mark had no gauge on the level of competition, other than a sense that because of the state of-the-art facilities, top-quality local teams would flock to Baseball Heaven, challenging the Cougars in a way the National Junior Baseball League had not. Mark was not disappointed; whether because the complex was an attraction or because the winnowing-out process due to aging left only the more talented and more serious players, the Baseball Heaven league was a big step up.

The Cougars' roster began to change. More originals dropped out, replaced by considerably higher-focused players, some of whom assumed a varsity high school career was a certainty, not to mention vague college athletic aspirations. Josh would be able to show what he had learned in his pitching lessons and hone his hitting skills playing third base-Mark's old position - in the games he was not on the mound. As Josh matured and became more sure of his abilities, and as he developed Mark's stubborn streak, on-field and in-dugout clashes between father and son became more frequent, so much so that Mark eventually decided that when Josh was on the mound and a conference was required, his assistant would represent him in the conclave.

With a season that included multiple games against the other three teams in the league, the Cougars developed their first true rival and bitter rivalry and their first true nemesis umpire.

If Long Island were a city divided into the "right" and "wrong" side of the tracks, the Cougars would have originated from the tonier side. The Long Island Legends, as they called themselves, clearly were from the "wrong" side, mostly the lower-middle-class communities of Mastic Beach and Shirley. For the Cougars, the Baseball Heaven league was a way station on the path to college. For the Legends, Baseball Heaven was the hope that they could be "discovered' by a professional scout and rescued from a future of dead-end, low-paying jobs post high school (if they made it that far). They had swagger in a Bowery Boys sort of way and an aura of illegitimacy: that all of their players qualified as being under the age limit was somewhat suspect. As one of the Cougar players noted to Mark, it appeared that some of the 15-year-olds had driven themselves to the games (the minimum driving age in New York being 17).

That the two teams would clash temperamentally was a given. That they would clash physically was inevitable.

It began with a battle over practice that established the baseline for the Cougars-Legends animosity. Each team was allotted limited practice time as part of a tight schedule at the complex. This was important because it would give the teams a feel of their new fields and learn whatever quirks might exist playing on the newly-installed turf, the wind conditions, and a sense of how and where balls would carry. At the first practice, the Legends overstayed their time, cutting into the Cougars', and exuded snark as they turned over the field. The sniping between the teams continued at a scrimmage that began to take on the aspects of a beanball war. And this was before the season actually began.

As the Cougars were building bile and animosity toward the Legends, they also were introduced to the umpire who would become the bane of Mark's Baseball Heaven existence. He was known to the Cougars, and apparently, it turned out, to the baseball and football worlds (he also refereed high school football) simply as Fat Ira.

Fat Ira may have been in shape in his younger years, but by the time he reached Baseball Heaven, many pounds had made friends with his physique, limiting either his ability, or his desire, to be mobile. He left the impression that when he reached into his pocket, it wasn't for a broom to sweep off home plate, but for a quick snack to tide him over until his next meal. The fact that he rarely left his anchored position behind home plate-and that he often tried to call plays on the bases, all of them, while leaning against the backstop-was the source of much bench jockeying by Mark, who, as was noted as far back as the Disney tournament, never shied from an opportunity to bait an umpire. And while Fat Ira's mobility had diminished, his hearing had not, and the only body part that had not thickened was his skin.

The upshot was that when Fat Ira umpired a Cougars game, it was much better than even money that Mark would be watching the final innings from the parking lot, having been ejected for some indiscretion that offended Fat Ira. Whether this served to motivate the Cougars was uncertain, but at least the clashes between umpire and coach provided entertainment for the spectators and players, especially since Mark did not go quietly as he took the long walk across the field to his car.

Cougars-Legends meetings weren't games, they were class struggles. And when the Cougars played the Legends and Fat Ira was behind the plate, the confluence of rival and nemesis produced some of the most bitter and bizarre games the Cougars would play, punctuated by unusual rulings drawing on obscure parts of the rule book and beanball and baserunning battles not usually seen in games played by high schoolers. The bad blood would carry over to the postgame handshake which, if it happened at all, continued the war of words rather than transmit well wishes.

Following one especially hard-fought game, won by the Cougars with some late-game heroics, a Cougar player who had been a major contributor to the victory made some intemperate remarks during the postgame handshake about one of the Legends' sisters (who also happened to be the coach's daughter). Understandably, this comment was not well-received by either the player or his teammates and a brawl broke out. As punches were being thrown on the pitcher's mound, Fat Ira was witnessing the fracas from his usual perch against the backstop.

When it was over-after the Baseball Heaven management had arrived but before the need for police to be called-Fat Ira, having not lifted a finger to break up the conflagration, helped identify the most culpable miscreants so suspensions could be handed out.

And so it went for the first three years of Josh and the other Cougars' high school years. In addition to seeing and appreciating Josh's development and success, especially in making the high school varsity as a junior (take that, middle school coach!), Mark took pride in finding not just players with developed talent, but in identifying the player who had undeveloped promise and who could blossom in the Cougars' lineup. One such player was a youth Mark was convinced would develop as a valuable third baseman and run-producing hitter. The youth's father, a Pakistani immigrant, was unconvinced. He had seen his son fail as a hitter and was skeptical of future success, but Mark convinced the father that he had identified a flaw in the son's swing that was easily correctible. Still skeptical, the father agreed to let his son play for the Cougars, at least until the time came for the lad to depart for his annual summer with family back home in the Old Country.

Mark was very supportive as he worked with the player on his hitting and the many other rough edges in his game. Gradually, but surely, he became a key contributor for the Cougars' as well as a leader in the dugout-a popular addition to the squad who interjected just the right amount of levity to keep the Cougars both focused and loose at the same time. Mark and the player's hard work finally paid off when, in a crucial league game on Father's Day, he hit a walk-off home run to secure the Cougars' victory. As he circled the bases, and as the team mobbed home plate to greet him, Mark dispatched one of the teammates to retrieve the ball from beyond the outfield fence. He gave it not to the player, but to the father who, beaming, had joined the team from the bleachers. Mark and the father exchanged smiles and the father thanked Mark profusely for his faith in his son's promise. The father would keep the ball and, when his son died tragically in a motorcycle accident a few years later, make it part of the memorial ceremony at his mosque. In death, even more than it had in life, baseball had formed a bond between a Pakistani father more versed in cricket than in baseball and his son.

As the games and seasons continued, an ennui was beginning to set in. Mark realized his time as a coach was nearing an end, as Josh was entering his senior year in high school and would soon be leaving for college. There was only one thing left to do.

It was time to take the Cougars on the road again.

\*\*\*

The last three months of the Cougars' existence would be spent in places far away from Baseball Heaven in Yaphank, among them Rehoboth Beach, Delaware; Hinsdale, Massachusetts, and State College, Pennsylvania.

Rehoboth Beach was a return trip, a second consecutive Memorial Day tournament against teams from New York, Delaware, Pennsylvania, and Maryland that was more a reward than a competitive challenge. The previous year, the Cougars had ventured to the oceanside Delaware resort community for a competition and enjoyed the experience so much that Mark signed them up again.

What made the tournament special was not the competition, but the bonding among parents and players made possible by the compact resort area that is Rehoboth Beach. With the exception of the playing fields, everything was within walking distance, including restaurants, a boardwalk, arcades (with games that included Skee-Ball and Pokereno and the type of coin-operated fortunetelling machine that was central to the plot of the film "*Big*" - throwbacks to the parents' youth and shades of Coney Island and Long Beach). With cell phones making it easier to keep tabs on the boys, it was possible for parents and players to go their separate ways. So, for example, when the parents dined at a local brew pub that manufactured Dogfish Head beer on the outskirts of the central business district, the team supped instead at Hooters on the Boardwalk, where their raging teenage hormones could revel in the scantily-clad waitresses.

The Cougars enjoying parent free time in Rehoboth. (Photo courtesy of the Akbar Family)

Josh led the charge among the players, essentially supplanting his father as the team leader off the field (make no mistake, it was still Mark's team on the field, at least until whatever time an umpire chose to eject him). It wasn't quite a passing of the torch, but it was an indication of the evolving relationship between father and son, a generational evolution marked by a changing of roles.

To be sure, the tournament had its baseball moments, including what may have been the greatest highlight, and greatest comeback in team history. Down 16 runs and needing to score seven in the bottom of the fourth to keep the game from being foreshortened because of the "mercy" rule, Mark gave one of his practically patent-pending motivational speeches in the dugout. The message was simple, and so was the goal: to keep fighting and score enough runs at least to extend the game another inning.

The team began chipping away. One run became two, and then three, and the momentum built as the Cougars piled hit upon hit. Suddenly, it seemed as if they could do no wrong. They reached the magic number to extend the game and kept going. They tied the score. They took the lead. They won the game. When it was all over, the opposing coach asked for permission to speak to the Cougars. He congratulated them for not giving up, for continuing to believe in themselves, noting that he saw the desire in the Cougars' eyes and that he had warned his team, even with the big lead, that the game was far from over. Even his team, demoralized as they might have been by such a crushing loss, shook the Cougars' hands with a sense of awe at what they had witnessed. It was perhaps Mark's finest moment as a coach.

Hand shake after Cougars amazing comeback in Rehoboth (Photo courtesy of the Akbar Family )

As spring turned to summer and what was for most of the Cougars' high school junior year concluded, Mark was faced with a decision: enter the team in the Baseball Heaven summer league or take the team to tournaments around the Northeast. The key factor in the decision was not baseball-related. As the players entered their senior year in high school, it made more sense to sign them up for tournaments where they could combine competing with college visits.

So when Mark signed the team up compete in a tournament at the Dan Duquette Sports Academy in Hinsdale, Massachusetts (a suburb of Pittsfield, if it is possible for a former small industrial city tucked away in the Berkshire Mountains to have a suburb), the goal was not just baseball. On the way, and on the way home, players and their families stopped to check out colleges, ranging from the University of Massachusetts in Amherst, the State University of New York at Albany and, for Josh, Springfield College and Westfield State College.

Josh and Mark knew a little about Springfield College and about Springfield itself: it was where Dr. James Naismith invented basketball in 1891 (fact, not legend, as is the story about Abner Doubleday, baseball, and Cooperstown) and became the home of the Basketball Hall of Fame. Mark and Josh would check out the college, but did not make it to the basketball hall.

They knew practically nothing about Westfield State. It was "discovered" for Mark and Josh by Mark's assistant coach, who in looking at colleges that might be near the tournament, found the school and realized it fit the profile for what Josh was seeking, including a strong graphic communications program and a Division III baseball team that might be interested in Josh as a pitcher. For Mark, the main attraction was that it was the alma mater of Peter Laviolette, who had just coached the National Hockey League's Carolina Hurricanes to the Stanley Cup championship. That alone was enough for a visit.

Mark and Josh toured both campuses, made their mental notes and continued on to Hinsdale. The Duquette tournament carried the attraction of a mix of participating teams with current college athletes-as karma would have it, players from both the Springfield and Westfield State baseball teams. They would regale Josh with tales about life on their respective campuses and with their teams and promised to pass the word back to their coaches about Josh's interest in their schools.

The Duquette tournament harkened back to Cooperstown: barracks lodging that allowed for one last collective living experience, team bonding pranks and shared bad taste practical jokes and insults. The disappointment was that because of bad weather, they were not able to play their scheduled game at Wahconah Park, a 1919-vintage stadium with wooden grandstands that is in the National Register of Historic Places.

College bound Cougars at the Duquette tournament. (Photo courtesy of Mark Rosenman)

A month later, the Cougars would play tournaments in a Philadelphia suburb, on the campus of Widener University, whose baseball field mimics the proportions of Fenway Park, with its "blue monster" as an homage to the Boston stadium's famed left - field wall, and at Penn State. They were two other college campuses for the team to visit; some additionally took in Temple University and other Philadelphia-area schools.

The Cougars meet the Blue Monster. (Photo courtesy of the Akbar Family)

And then, as summer turned to fall, the Commack Cougars' history came to an end. The team began their senior high school year, continued their college visits, filled out their college applications, and waited for their acceptances.

The Cougars would close the books book having played 361 games. They won 218, lost 134, and tied nine. There is no record of how many times Mark was ejected for arguing with umpires. Over the decade of the team's existence, 65 players would wear the Cougar uniform, including six who would span its entire history.

Of the 65, two would play Division I college baseball: the Cooperstown tournament ringer who, as was noted, reached the major leagues for half a cup of coffee, and a sometime Cougar , pitcher who would hurl briefly for a Long Island college before leaving the school. A few others would try out for, and even play, on Division III squads. And Matt Fleishman would play a few games for an independent league team.

Disney would continue to run big-time youth tournaments, and Cooperstown Dreams Park would continue to flourish, expanding to more teams and additional weeks. Lou Presutti Jr. would follow the Clete Boyer model, wintering in North Carolina and moving north for the Dreams Park Season. He would pass away in 2016, not having realized his dream of replicating Dreams Parks around the country (he built one in Port St. Lucie, Florida, but sold it). His son, Lou III, would take over the Cooperstown operation.

Baseball Heaven would prove less than divine for Andy Borgia,who, a few years after opening it, would sell his interest in the facility amid personal financial difficulties . It is still operating, under different ownership, and is realizing Borgia's vision of a facility that attracts top-notch youth reams and college and pro scouts. It partnered with former major leaguer Frank Catalanotto, who runs youth clinics and gives instruction there.

Fat Ira passed away in 2013. His obituary in *Newsday*, the local daily newspaper, said "he dedicated his life to making sure the rules of the game were firmly upheld."

Josh would go on to Westfield State, where he would major in communication arts. An injury would keep him from ever putting on a Westfield State baseball uniform. He interned with the public relations department of the Springfield Falcons, an American Hockey League affiliate of the Edmonton Oilers, "skating on the ice and throwing tee shirts into the crowd," Josh would note. Eventually, he would convince the Falcons management to let him work on videos and scoreboard graphics, which would lead to internships with the Brooklyn Cyclones, the New York Mets' New York-Penn League affiliate.

"He was talented with graphics, even in high school," Mark noted. "He did a lot of video work. He started a business where he was doing things, making recruiting videos for kids to send to colleges. As a parent, you're wondering: Is this a sustainable career? Then he got the internship with the Falcons and they loved him. It's a field that I didn't know much about. I didn't know what it paid. But he loved it, and so we encouraged it. He didn't really know what he wanted to do. Then he found this niche. He loved it. So we encouraged it."

After graduating from Westfield State, Josh got a job as a graphic artist at a magazine, and then the call came: Would he like to work full-time for the Mets, doing scoreboard videos and graphics?

"It was a dream job," Josh said. "I remember, when I got the job, I started crying. I called my dad. I said it was just a shock." Josh would succeed with the Mets and be promoted to supervisor in the graphics department. "It's an organization I love working for," he said.

The job would also give Josh the upper hand in conversations with his father. "I give him some trivia that I have been getting at work and see if he can answer it," Josh said. "Now I can tell him he's wrong. That's the big difference."

With Josh away at college, and the Cougars history, Mark had time on his hands. He used it to scratch an itch that had been unfulfilled since he graduated from college and set aside his dream to be a sports broadcaster, first to join his father's general contracting business and then as operations manager for a company manufacturing high-end furniture. He decided to start his own sports talk show, broadcasting over the Internet from his spare bedroom-the one with the sports memorabilia and his wife, Beth's, cookie jars. He developed a format that centered on live, longform interviews with sports personalities: former major-league athletes, mostly, and several sports book authors. Mark started the show as a solo act; a few months later, his former Cougars assistant coach ,who had been a sports editor at a newspaper, joined him as a co-host.

But that was only part of Mark's dream, and after a few years of *Wayne's World*-meets- David Suskind *OpenEnd*-meets *SportsCenter* broadcasting from the spare bedroom, Mark got the idea to take the show to terrestrial radio. He hit up some friends as sponsors, bought time on an AM station and *SportsTalk New York* was fully born. The move gave the show additional exposure, added credibility and cachet provided the needed backup for the next part of Mark's living-the-dream plan: the ability to obtain press credentials and join the established sports media. Instead of following his favorite teams as a fan, Mark could now cover the Rangers and Mets as part of the press corps –as a reporter for WLIE 540 AM radio.

Just as he had done decades before when working for the campus radio station at his college, New York Tech, Mark would record pregame interviews with players, mingle with the established beat reporters in the pregame mess, sit in the press box during the games, and join in the postgame news conferences. He filed video reports on the *SportsTalk New York* Facebook page and audio files on the show's website. He would proudly call his co-host every time one of his postgame press conference questions became the focus of the television reporters' recaps and the print reporters' stories.

Mark also eagerly established friendships with players, long since retired, who had been the heroes of his youth and the subject of some of those college radio station interviews. His thirst for those interactions, while not insatiable, increased exponentially. That led him to look for a vehicle through which he could meet and mingle with a broader spectrum of ex-players.

That's how he discovered New York Mets Fantasy Camp.

We'll delve a little deeper into the fantasy camp phenomenon later in this book, but in a nutshell, fantasy camp is a week in which frustrated former ballplayers who ended up as lawyers, accountants, and the like get to pretend that they are major-leaguers. They train and play in a major league facility under the tutelage of the coaches and players who did make it and who now spend a week imparting their knowledge to the wannabes and regaling them with stories. For the participants, the week is not cheap-in the neighborhood of $5,000, everything included-but how can you put a price on living a dream?

Mark wangled a press credential to cover Mets Fantasy Camp. He would get to talk to some of the participants, but also hang out with the former players, whom he would interview not only about the fantasy week but about their careers. He would ingratiate himself with the then-current Mets management, which would cement his press corps status and improve his access while covering the major league squad.

Mark paid his way to Port St. Lucie, Florida, site of the Mets' training compound, and convinced his oldest and best friend

Jeff Cohen, to join him as a photographer/videographer to help record Mark's interviews. Then, practically at the last minute, Jeff developed health issues and was unable to make the trip. Mark thought about who could replace Jeff, and the more he thought about it, the more the answer became obvious.

Josh.

Josh was still in college -on intersession between semesters --and the concept of working for the Mets was still years off. With the prospect of a free week in Florida instead of a New York or Massachusetts January, as well as a chance to polish his videographer skills, Josh agreed to join his father.

Josh eagerly watched how the campers when through their own "spring training," stopping at different stations for skills practice under the tutelage of former major leaguers. Josh got involved in some of the banter with longtime coach Joe Pignatano (an original Met, a catcher on the 1962 team, and a coach on the 1969 world championship team).

Josh moved on to watch one of the pitching stations. The instructor was former Mets reliever Turk Wendell. Josh and Mark would fondly remember an encounter with Wendell from years back, when Josh was still in Little League and Mark, Josh, and some of the Cougars visited spring training. After the workout, they joined a throng seeking autographs. As he walked from field to clubhouse, Wendell refused the pleadings from the youngsters - until one of them said, "Please." "That's what I was waiting for," Wendell remarked, smiling. He stopped and spent the next 20 minutes singing baseballs, marking himself as one of the "good guys."

As the clinic session ended, Josh picked up a ball and started throwing. It had been a few years since he had put on a uniform and competed, but some of the skills honed through years of lessons and high school varsity and Cougars games remained and he was able to display flashes of talent. As Josh broke off a curveball, Wendell noticed. Having spent the day with 40- and 50-somethings (the minimum age for participation being 30), Wendell was excited at the possibility of teaching someone barely into his twenties. He showed Josh different grips, and how to throw a knuckleball.

Josh was hooked.

He turned to Mark and said, "When I turn thirty, we've got to do this. We're doing this together."

Mark never forgot.

"When I turn thirty, we've got to do this" (Photo courtesy of Mark Rosenman)

So with Josh firmly settled in a job, a home of his own and a relationship (and with a wedding planned for the end of the next year), Mark and Beth decided to give Josh as a 30th birthday present what he had mentioned casually almost a decade before: a week with his father at Mets fantasy camp.

For Mark, it will be a bittersweet week, fueled by the realization that it will signal Josh's passage into the next phase of his life. "I kind of realized it's the last time I'll get to spend a full week with him," Mark said. "There's a new dynamic. He's a plus one, now, and then maybe there will be a plus one-and-a-half or two. After this, there's not going to be that time again, having spent all those years."

It will be in a slightly different level, but for Mark and Josh, the trip to Mets fantasy camp will be no different than for the other campers: a chance to turn back the clock and think about hopes, and dreams, and what might have been had fate not taken them in different directions.

And getting there would be part of the fun.

# CHAPTER 2

## THE HOUSE OF THE RISING SON

Some children are predestined to grow up and go into the family business. Whether it is a law firm, a restaurant or a contracting business, some parents cannot wait for the day when they can add "& Son" (or in the case of the famed New York City appetizing store, "& Daughters") to the business' name.

From a very young age, the children begin learning the ins and outs of their future line of work, sitting on the lap of their parent, becoming fixtures around the office. When they are of age, they become legacies at their parents' alma maters, intern at the family firm, and, if they want to branch out and sow their professional wild oats before returning to the fold, play on their family's professional connections to ensure that they find the right job and travel in the right circles.

Dad— or mom, as the case may be—is only too happy to make the introductions and proudly boast about how junior is a chip off old block and yes, it is only a matter of time before he or she activates the succession plan, gives junior the keys to the executive washroom, and rides off to a happy retirement.

For baseball players, the path is not that simple—both for father and son. Many more variables stand in the way of father-son major league combinations: interest on the part of the progeny; talent; competition; the fact that the father, except for rare instances, will be finished with his career before the son is ready to begin, in some cases, the most elementary level of youth baseball, and will be out of baseball and out of influence as the son comes of age; the limited number of major-league jobs and the inability to just create more. You get the idea.

All of which helps explain why, over roughly 140 years of major-league baseball, with just under 20,000 men who have played major-league ball, there have only been 248 father-son combinations, according to the Elias Sports Bureau. And that double counts fathers who had more than one make it to the bigs, such as Ray Boone and his sons Bret and Aaron or the Alomars—Sandy Sr. and his sons Roberto and Sandy Jr. Three generations? Even rarer—only five (the Bells, Boones, Colemans, Hairstons, and Schofield/Werths).

And the rarest of the rare: fathers and sons who get to play together in the same regular season lineup: only two—Ken Griffey Sr. and Jr. in 1990 and Tim Raines Sr. and Jr. in 2001.

"It was probably the biggest, most special moment of my baseball career," Hall of Famer Tim Raines Sr. recalled. "And we're talking about winning two world championships and all the other things in the game that I did."

It took some maneuvering to get Raines Sr. traded from the Montreal Expos to the Baltimore Orioles near the very end of his career, but it happened and allowed father to give his son the ultimate surprise on October 4, 2001. "By the time I got there, the team was on the field and getting ready for the game. So I went in, got my uniform on, and went on the field. And as my son was getting ready to do his sprints in pregame, I moved out in my uniform and it was like he saw a ghost when he saw me in the uniform. So that was probably the coolest thing that I ever really been through. It's something that you don't really think about, you don't feel like it's going to happen because one, you're a player, you don't have control where you play a lot of times and, or who you play with. Getting that opportunity was not only special, for me and my son, but also, knowing that the Expos and the Orioles gave us that opportunity is something I am very grateful for."

There is an asterisk to the Griffeys's and the Raineses's accomplishment: it was first achieved decades before, 1941 to be exact, in the Negro Leagues. Frank Duncan Jr., a catcher who won multiple Negro National League and Negro World Series titles as a player and manager of his hometown Kansas City Monarchs (he was Jackie Robinson's first manager) inserted his son Frank III into the lineup as his batterymate for a game. Frank III, not normally a pitcher, went the entire nine innings in a 2–1 Monarchs loss. Shortly afterward, they would carry togetherness a step further: both served in the Army in World War II.

Frank Duncan was the first to play professionally with his son.(Public Domain)

Seven years later, also in the Negro Leagues, the Wellses—Willie Wells Sr. and his son Willie Jr. would form the left side of the infield in a game for the Memphis Red Sox, with the son at shortstop and the father moving over from his usual position to man the hot corner.

And at the major-league level, Hal and Brian McRae did play together, in a spring training exhibition game, a few years before the Griffeys appeared in a game that counted. Brian was in his first major-league camp—he would not make the roster until a few years later. "It just happened that my dad was there and I got to play in a game with him," Brian said. "So that was a bonus ... It was a unique experience. I didn't know the significance of it until much later. I didn't know that no father and son had appeared in the game together. Even though it was a spring-training game, wasn't a regular-season game and the Griffeys would do that a few years later, but yeah, I was just really kind of caught up in the moment and I think my father was too and it was something that we didn't make that big of a deal about. We just happened to be in the right place at the right time and a lot was made out of it by other people, but to us at that time it wasn't that big of a deal."

Having his dad Hal play in the game was a "bonus" for Brian.(Photo courtesy of the Kansas City Royals)

Brian would get to have a somewhat different father-son experience when, in 1991, a year after he broke into the Kansas City Royals lineup, father Hal was named the manager. He spent three years playing for his dad. "I think it would've been biblical if I wasn't already there, but the fact that I was there before he got there, made it a little bit easier adjustment to go through," Brian said. "That's something that you go through with your son and travel ball. It's not an ideal situation in the majors. But you're in the big leagues and you're not going to complain about being in the big leagues playing for your dad."

One difference between fathers wanting their sons to follow them into law, or education, or accounting, compared to baseball players is that every day, or at least every home game, was Take Your Child to Work Day. Major-league fathers and their sons interviewed for this book were almost unanimous in their memories of youngsters spending time at the ballpark with their fathers, in the clubhouse, and on the field before games.

"In 1968, with the Cardinals, we had more kids in the clubhouse than we had players," said Dick "Ducky" Schofield, whose son Dick would follow him into the major leagues, as well as his grandson Jayson Werth. "It was just one of those good things. All the guys and kids would go back to an area inside the ballpark. It was a great big area and they'd be throwing balls and hitting balls back in there. I mean, it's a wonder they didn't kill somebody. They had a great time."

The fathers almost universally said they did not force baseball on their sons, but with few exceptions, did not discourage them if they said they wanted to pursue professional baseball as a career, although they felt it important to stress the difficulty of making it through college and the minor leagues and the perseverance required to make it and the focus needed to be successful on the big-league level.

One of the exceptions, apparently, was Ruben Amaro Sr., a shortstop who spent 11 years in the major leagues. "He didn't want either one of us, me or my brother, to go into baseball," Ruben Jr. said. "He wanted us to go on to be doctors or lawyers, or something like that. And when we both ended up going into baseball ... it was interesting."

While Ruben Sr. was hoping for a different career his sons, for Ruben Jr., there was no alternative: baseball was the only thing he knew. "He was the reason baseball was my whole life," Ruben Jr. said. "I knew nothing, really nothing else."

And, it should be noted, the relationship between father and son deepened after Ruben Jr.'s playing career when he went into the front office, rising to the position of general manager of the Philadelphia Phillies while his father was a minor-league instructor for the team. "It was fun being able to work," Ruben Jr. said. "It was just a pleasure to be around him and to be able to spend time to learn from him. There are so many other similar things off the field that I learned and about how to handle certain things, certain situations in the front office. I was able to bounce off a lot of things with him."

Perhaps the ultimate honor came when Ruben Jr. was asked to play his father on the television series *The Goldbergs*, produced by an old high-school classmate of his— an episode in which he is played by the son of another former major leaguer, relief pitcher Eddie Guardado. "It was an honor because my dad had passed away earlier in the year," Ruben Jr. said. "I felt very humble by being able to play him. It gave me a lot of pride and it was very, very nostalgic for me."

More than being part of the family business, multigenerational baseball families are part of an exclusive club. They know the special lingo and the secret handshake, as it were, and can converse on a level much different, and much deeper, than if they did not share a vocation. To that end, baseball formed, and continues to form, a lifetime bond that sets them apart from the rest of the work and even siblings who chose different careers.

This is what some of them had to say:

## MAURY AND BUMP WILLS

Maury Wills came late to the major leagues—he was close to 27 when he made his major-league debut with the Los Angeles Dodgers in 1959—but when the then-career minor leaguer was finally called up to replace the slumping Don Zimmer, his energy and exciting play took the major leagues by storm. He was a key contributor to the Dodgers' world championship that year. But it wasn't until the next year that he showed the talent that would be the hallmark of his career: his ability to steal a base. In his first full season, 1960, he became the first National Leaguer to steal 50 bases in 37 years, back to the waning days of the Deadball Era. Two years later, he would set a major-league record by stealing 104 bases, breaking Ty Cobb's deadball record of 96. He was so prolific a basestealer that the manager of the archrival San Francisco Giants ordered his grounds crew to water down the basepaths when hosting the Dodgers to slow Wills down.

He would go on to a 14-year, borderline Hall-of-Fame career in which he would bat .281 with 2,134 hits and 586 stolen bases; win the 1962 National League Most Valuable Player Award and win three world championships.

When Elliott Taylor "Bump" Wills was born in July 1952, Maury was in the middle of his second season with the Class D Hornell Dodgers, the then-Brooklyn team's farm club in the Pennsylvania-Ontario-New York League. Bump would celebrate his seventh birthday right around the time dad Maury was called up to the majors from the Dodgers' farm club in Spokane, Washington.

Bump's path to the major leagues differed from his father's: He went to Arizona State, where he was part of a squad that was twice the runner-up to national champion juggernaut USC (1972 and 1973). From 1971 to 1974, when he was at Arizona State, Bump shared the roster with 18 teammates who would also go on to the major leagues, most notably Alan and Floyd Bannister (no relation), Ken Landreaux, Craig Swan, and Jim Umbarger. Also on the roster was Danny White, who would make his mark in football, quarterbacking both at Arizona State and with the Dallas Cowboys.

Second baseman Bump was drafted by the Texas Rangers in the first round, sixth overall, in the January 1975 draft and his rise to major leaguer was meteoric compared to his father: He would make his major-league debut only three short years later, in April 1977. His major-league career did not come close to matching his father's, however, lasting only six years. The record books show him with a .266 average and 807 hits. He did follow in his father's footsteps as a basestealer, hitting a peak of 52 in 1978—still the Texas Rangers' record. He would play two additional years in Japan before retiring.

As a child, Bump Wills remembers, he did get instruction from his father—not in baseball, but in how to play the guitar. Maury Wills was a world-class banjo player—he appeared on television variety shows and spent 10 years as a lounge act in Vegas—and he passed on tips of playing the stringed instrument to his son in what would become a lifelong avocation for Bump. Most of what learned about how to pay baseball, and other sports, came from his two-year-older brother, Barry, a relationship that would become increasingly competitive over the years as they moved from elementary school through high school.

"He was a not only a good baseball player, but a smart baseball player," Bump recalled. "And so he would win the game in our competition probably 75 percent of the time and he would always do it late in games. It was about being smart, not just about talent ... So I grew up not trying to be my dad's son or to have a goal to be better than my dad. I had a goal of trying to be better than my brother, because he was that good."

While Maury was called up to Los Angeles, the rest of the family remained in Spokane, which is where Bump and Barry grew up. Maury did not get to see his sons play and, in the years before widespread televising of games, Bump and Barry could only listen to Vin Scully's radio word portraits.

Which is not to say that Maury did not have an influence on Bump. Each summer, he would get to spend three weeks with his father during a long homestand. He would get to wear a Dodgers uniform with his father's number on the back and get some instruction from Maury's teammates, most notably infielder Jim Gilliam. "He would have Jim Gilliam take me off to the side and show me some things about infield play because he didn't know how, being Maury Wills, he would react to me or, for that matter, how I would react to him. I'm sure he was standing off somewhere in the distance watching," Bump said. "My dad didn't start doing that as far as instruction until I was like a junior in high school when he knew I was at the age that I knew what I was doing and that I was listening to what he was saying."

If there was a watershed moment in their relationship—one

that both Bump and Maury remembered fondly—it came that year, when Bump was a high school junior, during one of the three-week stints in Los Angeles. By now, Bump had grown to his father's size and build. He was on the field, wearing the uniform with his father's name and number on the back, as the pregame infield practice was about to start. "They have [Steve] Garvey at first, [Davey] Lopes was there, Bill Russell at short, Steve Yeager, you know who they are. My dad and they were ready to go take pregame infield, and my dad walked up to me and said, 'Hey, I've got to do this radio spot here right now. Can you fill in for me?' And I remember thinking, so I told him yeah, I can take it. Done that my whole life, you know, I could take infield. And so I was out there with those guys, the starting lineup, and I was at shortstop with Bill Russell. And I took a flawless infield like we always do before the game. And as I walked off the field, some portion of my brain in my head said, I can play with these guys ... the next year I went to college and I just remember that my confidence proved so much at that moment that when I went to college I had more of a thought pattern of maybe I can get to the big leagues."

Taking flawless infield with Dodgers gave Bump confidence.(Photo courtesy of Bump Wills)

"He handled himself very well," Maury recalled. "The fans didn't even know the difference. Walter Alston, my manager, never said the kid can't go out there, he's not doing it right. That was pressure on him, I kind of pushed him to do it."

Decades later, Bump would ask Maury about that time: "Did you do it on purpose or was there really a radio spot, something you had to do? And he just winked at me and said, 'I knew what I was doing.' And so he had set that up and he didn't have a radio spot. He just watched me from around the corner take infield. And that was a great moment."

Maury remembers another moment, in which Bump appeared on the field as himself. Bump was on the field with his father, who was being honored by the team. "I'm at a ceremony which preceded the game at Dodger Stadium," Maury said, "I was voted the most valuable player on the team, or the most popular. For that, I received an automobile, a two-seater convertible, a nice little car, and I gave it to Bump, and he drove it through the center-field gates all the way to Arizona State in Tempe. That was a nice moment for me."

Maury finally got to see Bump play in college but did not get to see Bump's first major- league game, in Baltimore against Hall of Fame pitcher Jim Palmer. Maury was otherwise engaged, managing the Seattle Mariners. He would see Bump play a short time later, when the Mariners went to Seattle for a series.

"They came to Seattle to play," Maury said. "He was all over the place. He just took over. He was getting hit after hit, stealing bases, going from first to third on base hits, scoring runs. He just ruined us. I was proud and embarrassed at the same time. Being my son, I took him back to the hotel after the game. He got in the car, and I yelled at him, 'Jeez, why don't you play like that all the time?' I think it was a big moment for him, too."

Maury did keep track of Bump's progress from afar, and Bump would occasionally call his father for advice when he was in a slump. "He must have known I wasn't going good because I'm sure he was checking me out in the newspaper and I was in a slump," Bump said. "And so I called him and without telling him why I was calling, he already knew. And so he directed the conversation to the psychological part of the game: that when you're in a slump, you have to be able to shake it off, come back and just keep battling ... that helped me have the right perspective, a different perspective. I loosened up. I go a hit that night. The next day I got an RBI game-winning hit, played good on defense. The next day I got two hits and I was on my way to a hot streak.

"Dad to me was always just dad, my father, not Maury Wills this world-famous baseball player who's got three World Series rings," Bump said. "To me, now I know how good he was and how valuable he was. But he was just my dad. I didn't necessarily want to be a Major League Baseball player. I just played the game because I liked it and I liked to compete and I was good at it. And if I didn't become a major-league player, that was okay with me because I had other things on my mind besides just being a good athlete."

But being a major leaguer did create a special relationship between him and his father. "Major League Baseball is a fraternity, and it's a lifetime fraternity and it's an endless fraternity," Bump said. "The thing I feel most proud of is that I belonged to that fraternity. And when my dad and I would talk when I was in major-league ball, right through from the beginning, from my first year in the big leagues until my last, I would talk to my dad. And the conversation's changed, where he and I could have a conversation as father and son, but then in the next breath we could also have a conversation as ex-major-league baseball players. There's a certain mindset and jargon that goes along with being a major-league baseball player. And I found myself on the same level, the same level as my dad and all those guys who played the game before. And to me that was really exciting."

Maury concurred that the relationship between him and Bump was special because of baseball. "Not that I love him more than I love his brother, it's just that we were both major- league baseball players. We had a language and an experience that paralleled one another," Maury said. "His brother, Barry, was a better baseball player, a better athlete, than Bump. But Bump had something inside of him that got him to be a professional baseball player that his brother did not have.

"I say this with a lump in my throat. His brother said he didn't want to play major-league baseball because saw his father going away every year to play baseball, and he's sitting home waiting. He said he wanted to get married some day and he didn't want his wife sitting home waiting for hm all the time, but that's the life of a baseball player. That's a rough one for me to recall."

## THE WALLACHS

Tim Wallach had a 17-year major league career, most of it on Montreal Expos teams that also included Hall of Famers Gary Carter, Andre Dawson, and Tim Raines. A slick-fielding third baseman, his stat line shows a lifetime batting average of .257, 260 home runs, 1,125 runs batted in, three Gold Gloves and five All-Star selections. While not Hall-of-Fame numbers, he was selected as the Expos' Player of the Year three times and was elected to the Canadian Baseball Hall of Fame.

Tim has three sons—Matt, born in 1986; Brett, born in 1988;

and Chad, born in 1991 — and with the end of his playing career in 1996, he would get to coach all of them at different age levels, and all three would follow in their father's footsteps by going into professional baseball. Two — Matt and Chad — would also attend their father's alma mater, Cal State Fullerton.

Matt, a catcher, was drafted in the 22nd round by the Los Angeles Dodgers in 2007 and spent seven years in the minor leagues, rising briefly to AAA in 2013. Brett, a pitcher, was drafted in the third round by the Los Angeles Dodgers in 2009. He didn't advance past A ball over four minor league seasons.

Chad, also a catcher, has had the most success. Drafted in the fifth round by the Miami Marlins in 2013 and traded a year later to the Cincinnati Reds, he was promoted to the majors in 2017, where he played in six games. In the offseason, the Marlins claimed him back. He played with the major-league club briefly at the beginning of the 2018 season and again after the September callups and is slated to be the Marlins' backup catcher for 2019, where, when he is not in the lineup, he can sit next to the Marlins' bench coach — his father, Tim.

Tim is especially proud that he was able to coach all three of his sons.

"It's just time, that's what it's all about," he said. "You spend time with your kids, however you do it. As long as you're spending time with them, you create that father-son bond — relationships that carry on and keep it close forever."

For Chad, the bond created by father coaching son was cemented long before he was able to understand and appreciate his father's major-league career. "It all started in the travel ball scene," Chad said. "He was my coach, and when we'd go to tournaments it was just weird because coaches of other teams would be coming up to him to get autographs and whatnot. I think that's kind of when I realized like how big of a deal he was and how good his career was. The more I'm around baseball and see how hard it is to do what he did during his career it just makes it that much more impressive. "

"He was always encouraging," Chad noted. "He never pushed too much on things. Like he would kind of wait for me to ask questions, but knowing that he'd been through all of this kind of stuff, I was always asking questions and he was always there to help. So it was really nice having somebody that had been through it and experience things the same way I had."

The bond was extended by sharing the college experience. "You go back to what my roots were and go watch him play at the same place," Tim said. "Obviously, a different field, but a newer, better field, but it was pretty cool just being able to sit there and watch him kind of grow and become who he is now. "

Tim also got to see two Chad milestones—his first major league at-bat (playing for Cincinnati) and his first home run (for the Marlins). "None of my home runs ever felt as good as watching him hit his first," Tim said.

Having his father there made it special for Chad, too. "It was such a cool moment not just to be able to hit my first home run and get a couple of hits, but to have your dad there in the dugout with you. "

"It was awesome having a dad who played in the major leagues growing up and then to be able to follow in his footsteps," Chad said. "In college, you got to see and hear some of the stories that went on with him there. And being able to play for him now is probably the coolest part, just because I know not too many people have had that opportunity, so it's pretty cool to be able to say I'm one of those people who have done that."

"You just pass whatever you can down to help him just be a good baseball player," Tim said, "Just to be a good young man and father some day and husband, that's the most important thing." But it is rewarding to share with Chad his baseball knowledge and the major- league experience. "It's what I know and now it's what he knows and we can talk about whatever situations and whatever it is that need to be talked about, and he knows that I know what I'm talking about I want him to be the best he can be at whatever he does, and it just so happens it's baseball."

Tim and Chad Wallach.( Photo courtesy of Mark Rosenman)

## ED AND BOBBY CROSBY

Ed and Bobby Crosby both had relatively brief and modest major- league careers. They were both infielders; Ed was a shortstop who switched to second base while Bobby made the big leagues at his father's original position and stayed there. Ed spent all of parts of six seasons with the Cardinals, Reds, and Indians. By the time Bobby was born in 1980, Ed had retired, having spent three seasons in the minors after his major-league career ended and before starting a career as a scout.

Bobby's rookie major-league season was his most successful —he was named Rookie of the Year in 2004, his first full season, with the A's. He would play eight major-league seasons with the A's, Pirates, and Diamondbacks. His career statistics: .236 batting average, 62 home runs and 276 runs batted in, all better than his father's .220/0/44 stat line.

Ed has two other sons. One, Blake, played college baseball and was drafted by the A's but did not make it to the majors (he currently works in baseball, scouting for the Toronto Blue Jays). The other, Brian, did not play college or professional ball but instead went into animation and is currently the creative director for Marvel Themed Entertainment.

"Growing up, I thought it was the coolest thing ever that my dad played in the major leagues," Bobby said, counting among his childhood memories not only playing catch with his father but also accompanying him to games, where they sat in the stands with other scouts and as a treat, Ed let Bobby work the radar gun. "I didn't have the clubhouse kid atmosphere, but I had the scouting kid's atmosphere."

Ed feels he had a good relationship with all three sons and was close to them despite being divorced from their mother. "I never pushed baseball on any of my sons," he said. "Of course, I wanted them to play, but they were pretty good in all sports. Especially Bobby. Bobby was one hell of a soccer player. He played ice hockey. I didn't know if he was going to go for baseball or be a weekend warrior and go for other sports. I think it was his junior year in high school, he really decided he wanted to concentrate on baseball."

While Ed didn't push Bobby, he was supportive, an approach Bobby appreciated. "He encouraged me to do whatever I wanted to do, and when I said I wanted to play in the big leagues, he was very encouraging, but he wasn't pushing. I think that's why I continue to have love for the game, because he didn't push me to go play ... He was always there to pitch to me. He was always there to play catch. He was always there to hit me ground balls, but it was never something we had to do."

As Bobby honed his baseball skills, scout Ed began realizing that his son was a major- league prospect. "I thought he was a kid who was going to get drafted. I didn't know where, but I definitely thought he was going to get drafted," Ed said. Bobby was drafted, but chose to attend college at Long Beach State—where, he noted, Ed attended his games and would leave notes in his car afterward, consoling him about errors and offering positive reinforcement. Bobby eventually was a first-round selection of the Oakland A's.

Ed continued to follow Bobby through his minor-league career and was in the stands in Las Vegas when Bobby got the call to the majors. In fact, Bobby changed into street clothes and broke the news to Ed and his mother himself. Not wanting to miss his son's major league debut, Ed and a friend got into a car and began driving from Las Vegas to Oakland. "It was special to see him out on the big-league field, an amazing feeling," Ed said.

Sadly, while Bobby made it onto the A's roster, his first game appearance came on the road—across the country in Baltimore. But a year and a half later, after Bobby's successful first full season, Ed was in the stands when Bobby received his Rookie of the Year award. "Someone took a picture of my dad standing up, watching me," Bobby said. "I could see on his face everything he was thinking.' It is Bobby's favorite photo of his father.

"I was very proud, cheerful," Ed said. "I'm an emotional guy, anyway. I was just a very fulfilling feeling as a father to see your son go through that and be nominated for such an award."

Looking back, Bobby agrees with his father that all three Crosby sons had close relationships with their father. But baseball, he thinks, made his even closer. "I know that whatever I did, my dad would support me, but having him play and then I played, and how we talked after every single game, I can't imagine a different relationship that what we had. ...The fact that I was doing something that's what he knew and that was his life, and we could bond on that for however many years until I was thirty-something and stopped playing. I can't see it being stronger with me doing something else if I didn't play baseball."

Ed and Bobby Crosby. (Photo courtesy of Ed Crosby)

## DON AND DAMON BUFORD

Don Buford's mark on baseball was as a leadoff hitter, a spark plug who had a knack for getting on base by an assortment of means with a little bit of pop in his bat. Over a 10-year period, he played for the Chicago White Sox and the Baltimore Orioles, where he became a favorite of manager Earl Weaver and became the first player to lead off a World Series with a home run, off Tom Seaver in the 1969 fall classic. He finished with a stat line of a .264 batting average, 93 home runs and 418 runs batted in.

Damon, the youngest of three Buford boys, was born in the middle of father Don's time with the Orioles, and the only one to fully follow in his father's footsteps, playing baseball at USC and making it to the majors, starting with the Orioles. His brother Don Jr. played four seasons in the minors before getting his medical degree and becoming an orthopedic surgeon and Daryl never played professional baseball; his involvement with the sport came after he graduated from law school and became a sports agent. Damon's stat line: nine major-league seasons, .242 batting average, 54 home runs and 218 runs batted in with the Orioles, Mets, Rangers, Cubs, and Red Sox.

Don Buford never forced baseball on any of his sons, although he did make sure they knew the basics. "When they were growing up, as I talked baseball, and as we practiced baseball, I always gave the kids basic fundamentals—just have confidence and teach them to just have confidence in themselves and in their own abilities to be successful. There was no pressure put on them to play. My feeling was, you don't have to play baseball. If you are interested in other sports, or if you're not interested in sports, don't play. It kind of evolved over all three of my sons. My oldest one ended up playing college ball and then playing two [actually, four] years professional in the Oriole organization. He was going to med school at the same time, so the conversation I had with him was that you can be a doctor for life, you can't play baseball forever. So I think that it's better that you continue on with your medical, which is what his goal was and his desire, even in high school.

"And my middle son said, dad, I don't think I want to play baseball, and I said, great. So he says, I want to be an attorney. So he went to law school, and passed the bar, and he's a lawyer.

"And then Damon wanted to play baseball, so he ended up playing baseball. They had their own careers, and I was just encouraging them, and backing them, and being supportive of whatever they wanted to accomplish."

Damon's memories of baseball, his childhood, and his father came mostly from the offseason, when Don was home for the winter and not traveling. But he and his brothers did benefit from their father being a major leaguer, at least when it came to equipment.

"I don't think he ever bought me a glove or something like that," Damon said, "It was just something he brought home from the clubhouse. I always looked forward to seeing him when he got home at the end of the season or seeing him during the season. It was always new stuff, baseballs or gloves or bats ... One of the things I remember the most, I was like eight years old. My oldest brothers, they were probably 11 and 12 at the time. And it was the wintertime. He was home, and for whatever reason, the school bus didn't pick us up in the front yard, not because of weather or anything, like it just broke down or something and we found a trash bag, a big green trash bag in his office and we opened it up. It was all this fan mail that he hadn't opened for like five, six, seven years. We got in there and opened all these fan letters and all these baseball cards and back then it was the Bazooka bubble gum and all that stuff. That was one of the days when you realize for your dad's actually playing baseball ... Before then , I didn't really understand what he was doing. It was just, my dad went to work."

As for instruction, Damon said, it wasn't until he was in high school that his father began showing him the finer tricks of the trade. "My whole life, we never really talked about being good or bad or indifferent about baseball," Damon recalled. "I remember my junior year in high school, I had a pretty good year and when he came home from the season that year he said, 'I want to show you a couple things about bunting.' And that was really the first time he really showed me, taught me anything about hitting before ... It was never really talking about going to the big leagues or anything because I think he knows how tough the road is or how tough the road was and is and all that good stuff. ...We kind of had some conversations more so about life than baseball."

But making it to the major leagues gave Damon a greater appreciation of his father's road to the big leagues—becoming the first African American on the USC baseball team, dealing with segregation and discrimination. "There's a level of a relationship that no one else can really understand unless you played in the big leagues."

One odd part about being a major leaguer's son—and one who continued to work in baseball after his playing days ended—is that Don, who was working in the Orioles front office at the time, knew before Damon about his call-up to the big leagues. "Of course, I didn't tell him," Don said. "I wanted him to get that feeling of being called up and being told. And I didn't want him to think it was because of me. He earned it, and that's what I wanted him to realize, that he worked hard."

Both Damon and Don played for USC and the Orioles.(Photo courtesy of Damon Buford)

Fast forward to Damon's post-baseball career, which included running clinics and calling on his father to help—bringing home the link baseball had forged between the two. "It's kind of funny," Damon said, "because I was still leaning on him to help me run the clinic and here he is in his eighties. Can you take over? So it's kind of funny how the relationship, father son, it hadn't really changed."

One of the highlights of that clinic: Don and Damon having a catch—with a noticeable difference from when Damon was a child. "It was a great feeling," Don said. "Because I used to throw it, and he'd miss it, and I'd kid him: 'Now you're not chasing the ball like you did when you're a kid, you know how to catch it.'

"So we, have a lot of camaraderie, talking baseball and, the experiences that we both had playing and I know some of the experiences he had and difficulties, but it very seldom did he ever call and say, Dad, what am I doing or what do I need or anything like that. Because I tried to prepare him. I had time for the things that he had to face."

## TRIPLE PLAYS: THE BOONES, THE BELLS AND THE SCHOFIELDS

While there have been a considerable number of father-son major-league combinations, considerably rarer—rarer than a triple play—are families in which three generations made it to the bigs. Which make the Boones, the Bells, and the Schofields the rarest of the rare.

Ray Boone spent 13 years in the major leagues, from 1948 to 1960, with six teams. Originally a catcher, he switched to the infield at the request of his first major-league manager, Cleveland's Lou Boudreau, and spent his entire career in the infield, starting as a shortstop and later moving to third base and then to first. His stat line: .275 batting average, 151 home runs and 737 runs batted in. Son Bob—born the year before his father made it to the majors—followed in his father's footsteps as a backstop, but unlike his dad, remained behind the plate for his entire 18-year major-league career, playing for three teams and amassing a stat line of .254, 105 home runs, and 826 runs batted in. Bob's sons Aaron and Bret both had major-league careers. Bret, born three years before his father's major-league debut, was the trailblazer. In 1992, when he debuted with the Seattle Mariners, he became the first third-generation major leaguer. A power-hitting second baseman, he played for six clubs over the next 14 years, hitting .266 with 252 home runs and batting in 1,021 runs. Younger brother Aaron, born the year after his father broke in with the Philadelphia Phillies, played for six major-league teams over 12 years, starting with the Cincinnati

Reds, where on the last day of the 1998 season, he was part of the only infield composed of two sets of brothers: Bret at second and Aaron at third, flanked by the Larkins—Stephen at first and Barry at shortstop. Aaron's final stat line was a .263 average, 126 home runs, and 555 runs batted in.

Of note about the Boone family: all four were All-Stars, and all remained in the family business after their playing days. Ray spent over three decades as a Red Sox scout; Bob managed the Kansas City Royals and Cincinnati Reds; Bret worked as a minor-league instructor for the Oakland A's and Aaron, after a stint in the broadcast booth, landed a job as manager of the New York Yankees. And yes, there is a possibility of a fourth generation of Boones to play major-league ball: Bret's son Jake was drafted by the Washington Nationals in 2017 but chose to attend Princeton University, where he is on the baseball team and hopes to be in the 2020 draft, the next time he is eligible.

The Bell family dynasty began in 1950, when patriarch Gus broke in with the Pittsburgh Pirates. An outfielder, he would spend 15 years in the majors, most memorably with the Cincinnati Reds (and as a member of the 1962 original New York Mets starting outfield that had among them 19 children), batting .281 with 206 home runs and 942 runs batted in. Buddy, born in 1951 when Gus was with the Pirates, played 18 seasons with four teams, mostly at third base, batting .279 with 201 home runs and 1,106 runs batted in. Like the Boones, the third generation of Bells counted two major leaguers, both third basemen like their father. David, born while his father was playing for the Cleveland Indians, spent 12 years in the majors with six teams, producing a stat line of .257, 123 home runs and 589 RBIs. Younger brother Mike played briefly for the Reds in 2000.

Again, like the Boones, the Bells remained in baseball post-playing career. Gus worked as a scout for the Cleveland Indians and Texas Rangers; Mike is the director of player development for the Arizona Diamondbacks; and Buddy and David have become fifth father-son pair to manage in the major leagues, Buddy with the Tigers, Rockies and Royals, and David with the 2019 Reds.

Gus sits atop the Bell baseball family tree.(Photo courtesy of Manny&#039;s Baseball Land via tradingcarddb.com [Public domain])

The Schofield lineage spans three generations but is not as direct as the Boones and the Bells. John Richard Schofield, called Dick on his baseball card and Ducky by his teammates, played shortstop for seven major-league teams over 19 seasons, remaining in the bigs mostly because of his fielding; his stat line is a .227 batting average, 21 home runs and 211 runs batted in. His son, Richard Craig Schofield, also called Dick, and also a shortstop like his father, spent 14 seasons with four teams, batting .230, hitting 56 home runs and knocking in 353. The third generation came by way of Ducky's daughter, Kim, a champion sprinter and long jumper who competed in the 1976 Olympic trials. Her son, Jayson Werth, played the outfield for four major league teams over 15 seasons, batting .267 with 229 home runs and 799 runs batted in.

Werth, who retired in 2017, is not working in baseball—not yet, anyway. Grandfather Ducky did not remain in baseball. Uncle Dick did manage in the minor leagues.

It's probably no surprise that when dad works in a profession that takes him away from the family for long stretches of time, other relatives step into fill the void and hold the space until dad comes home. So when you ask Bret Boone who taught him about baseball, he responds that it was largely his grandfather Ray.

"I would say grandpa was probably my earliest influence in the game," Bret said, "I mean, he's the one that I used to bug. He tells the stories. I think we remember me waking him up at five in the morning, putting on the catcher's gear... He tells me that I was relentless, getting him out of bed, and you got to go play ball, gramps. He fills me in on what it was really like."

"I used to get this question asked constantly, you know, when I was a young player going through the minor leagues going through high school, college: How much did it help you growing up in a family where your grandfather, your dad [played major-league ball], and my answer is simple. I don't know how much it helped me, if any, but I do know that it didn't hurt me. I think that's a fair answer. I don't see any negative side to growing up that way, but the bottom line is you can play or you can't play. I could put thousands of kids through that childhood, and if you're not born with a certain something, it doesn't matter. You're going to go get a job like everybody else."

David Bell detailed a similar relationship with Grandpa Gus. "We had a really close relationship and he did fill in those gaps and when my dad was still playing," he said. "My dad played until I was signed, so there were times in high school my dad didn't see us, see me play much if ever. My grandpa was there at all the games throughout the first few years and playing in the minor leagues and he was there all the time. We were kind of like a best friend relationship that has two dads. "

Which made it even more important that David got tell an ailing Gus Bell that he had been called up to the major leagues. "My grandfather was really sick at the time and so that was a really neat call for me to make. And about a week or two after I got called up, I think the first time I was called up, he had a heart attack and he was not doing well. I only had a couple of at-bats, but knowing that he knew that I had made it was really, really special for me. He passed away a couple of weeks after that, after I got called up. "

"He knew I knew how much it meant, at least I really sensed that it was important to him, too, even in his battle. That was probably my biggest memory is that month or so. And then I went back [to the minors] and got called back up later. Memories are really good."

Gus Bell, he said, "was like the most positive person I've ever been around and I think he knew how much we loved the game and he sensed that we wanted to play. I think he had a big influence on me in understanding how important it is to stay positive."

Common to the Boone and Bell households was the role that the family business played in their upbringing and the ties among himself, his father, and his siblings.

"We all have a close relationship and looking back I really would have to say that that baseball played a key role and has our entire life with keeping us close," David Bell said. "And the reason I say that, as you know, we all go through different stages in our life ... and baseball was the one constant that we always had to go to. And even when you know you're a stubborn kid, and you're fighting your parents on something, the one thing that we always had in common was that language of baseball. It was the one thing we always kind of agreed on. It was the thing we could go to when we didn't have anything else to talk about. We always talk about baseball to this day. "

"Everything in our life, the core of it was baseball," according to Bret Boone. That included father Bob encouraging his sons to follow his career path. "He was always very supportive, encouraging. He never pushed me—I remember him doing an interview 25 years ago, and he was right on. He said, 'I never pushed my kids into playing baseball, but of course was happy when they were, that that was their passion.'

"And in my case, it I was dad, I'm going to USC and studies are important ... but my attitude was, I'm going to USC to play baseball, and give me the classes that I need and tell me what I need to stay eligible. That was my attitude going in, and a very naïve attitude. It ended up working out for me, but I can still remember college counselors calling me in and saying, hey, Bret, what are you plans after college? What do you want to pursue, what are your interests? And I said, I don't have any interests, I'm going to be a baseball player and I'm going to play in the big leagues for 13 years. And they'd look at me like, OK, that's great and, and you're on that track, but what if it doesn't happen? As I was looking at him, like, do you know who you're talking to? I am already, because it's already done in my mind. I truly believed that. It was naïve, and I can laugh at that 18-year-old kid. I'd walk into a restaurant and if everybody in the restaurant didn't know who I was or how great I was going to be ... I laugh at that guy, because he had no idea how hard it was to be a big-league player."

There is near unanimity among second-generation major leaguers that their fathers did not force them to play baseball—and the fathers tended to agree they left the decision up to their sons, pressure-free. Which is not to say they didn't care about how their progeny were doing and that they weren't proud of their sons' career choice.

Ducky Schofield spoke about having a rare opportunity to watch his son Dick play in a Little League game on an off-day for him. "He was a pitcher and he struck out all nine guys and the guy coaching the team took him out of the game, and he is sitting on the bench and I'm thinking that's just not right. I asked my wife why, why is he not playing? They said he can only pitch so many innings, and then they've got to take him out of the game. I said no, no, he's got to play someplace else after he pitches. I said, I've got to leave because I'm going to say something I shouldn't ... I think I talked to the guys and said, you know, like after you take him out of the game pitching, I said, I think you should play him in the infield. I just let it go at that. I was trying to be nice, but I was more upset that nice."

"As a young kid, he could play shortstop and he would always catch the ball and you know, it was just that he liked to play. I never made him play, he always would come to me and we used to go have batting practice. I'd hit him balls and his two sisters would shag balls for us. My dad did the same thing with me. He taught me how to play and I tried to teach Dick how to play baseball, not so much hit, field, and whatever, but to know how to play."

That relationship made it even more special for Ducky when Dick made it to the major leagues. Ducky was there. "When he ran out of the dugout to take the field, I mean, I don't know about anybody else, but it was probably the biggest thrill I've ever had in baseball ... Just to get out of the dugout an run to shortstop ... it wasn't hoping anymore, but he really was there and had done it. So I'll remember that I got to see his first hit. I got to see his first home run. That's a pretty special."

And to see his grandson—the son of one of the daughters who used to shag flies when Ducky threw to Dick—also become a major leaguer? "That's pretty neat," he said.

So far, a dynasty hasn't reached a fourth generation, but just as Bret Boone became the first third-generation major leaguer, his son Jacob could become the first to be the fourth in a major-league line. And if he makes it, both father and grandfather will have had a role in guiding his path.

Bret will have prepared Jake for the cerebral part of the game, and to him the important part is "encouraging you, teaching you how to be a man, and when times are tough, to give personal advice,what you went through. And I do that with my son. I'm really excited that my son's completely different than me. He's more of a realist. He's a freshman at Princeton, and a shortstop and he's going through a little tough time right now with the adjustment. But I said, listen, you're at the most prestigious academic institution, maybe in the world. You're doing well in school. You're starting as a freshman. I said, you're way ahead of the game, man. I said just keep grinding. It's going to be a learning process.

"I like talking to him about the mental side of the game and just reflecting on stuff I've gone through and I've passed that down to him. A lot of times with his swing, he goes to my dad for that and that's better, they have a different relationship  My dad's pretty good at knowing Jacob's swing, so they work on the physical side of the swing together more than me and him do, you know, I just talked to him about the mental side, how to prepare, what to think, what these guys are thinking."

As for the possibility of a fourth generation of Boones? "I reflect on it and you know, it's cool," said Bret, "because I had a great, great relationship with my grandfather and like they said he was a real early influence on me. But nowadays, you know, being 49 years old, I looked around and see, wow, this is pretty awesome. I never thought of that, it's the Boone family, you know, it's like, no, it's my dad, it's my gramps. So it's no big deal. But when you step back and look after your career's over on what we've accomplished as a family, it's just not a pump-your-fist-high-five. It's just kind of a smile of wow, this is pretty special what we've done starting with Grandpa and then dad and then me and then my brother. And then uh, you know, having a son that's in college baseball and who knows?"

## MARK CARREON

Camilo Carreon, a catcher, appeared in 354 games over parts of eight major-league seasons (only three of them full ones) with the Chicago White Sox, Cleveland Indians, and Baltimore Orioles, hitting .264 with 11 home runs and 114 runs batted in. His son Mark was born in 1963, Camilo's best season with the ChiSox. Mark made the majors in 1987—having been called up the day Camilo died (more about that later)—and spent 10 years with the New York Mets, Detroit Tigers, San Francisco Giants, and Cleveland Indians. His stat line: .277 average, 69 home runs and 289 runs batted in.

Mark Carreon describes his relationship with his father as "distant but close."

"We really became closer when I became a professional—we had that connection. But growing up, we were busy playing organized sports and busy doing our thing and he was working and coming home and tending to the yard."

But unlike many of the players interviewed for this book, Carreon does have vivid memories of his first catch with his father. "It was really one of my highlights of my childhood," he said. "He was real instrumental in many ways as far as providing an environment for us, when they signed us up to play organized ball at an early age and my brothers and I were allowed to play ball in the house and the backyard, breaking lamps and rolling up socks with rubber bands or making tape balls ... But one day in particular, my dad and I played catch and he used one of his old catching mitts. The way he would throw and receive the ball I thought was pretty impressive because I knew I was playing catch with an ex-major leaguer and just to watch his old form. I know his shoulder was probably hurting [the injury that shortened Camilo Carreon's major league career], it was fine. It was real fun. It was a moment that I embrace and I'll never forget."

"One of the most important things I remember about him is that he never pushed. He never pushed just because he played MLB. He knew that we were individuals and that we were going to pursue our own dreams. It just so happened that I did want to play. The way his approach was, he never forced us to follow in his footsteps. And I think that's the reason that I ended up loving the game was because of that approach, that kind of, I guess cautious and I don't know what the word is for that, but he was real. He kind of took a step back. I mean, he coached us and all but, it wasn't forced upon us and kind of like what I did to my boys, and it kind of turned them off. And then now that I look back at it, his approach was a method that allowed me to follow up with the game."

Growing up in Tucson, Arizona, where the Indians trained, Mark remembers going to spring training games with his father and meeting Frank Robinson and Boog Powell, as well as the family having fellow catchers Pat Corrales and Doc Edwards over for dinner. He remembers hanging out in the clubhouse, and going home with gifts of hats, T-shirts and Indians memorabilia.

"And then we got to walk on the field," he said. "And that was quite an introduction. That was his way of introducing the game to us. So with all that said I think that that approach was so important, because I think that with my kids, I made the mistake of being too fundamental, you know, and taking the fun away from the game is essentially what I did. Wanting to practice all the time and showing them the proper mechanics and this and that. I inadvertently was taking the fun out of it and they were just kids. So that's probably why they lean towards football. It was more of what they accomplished and without dad partaking in that.

"But he allowed me to take it all at my pace and he instilled in me that baseball is a game and games are meant to be fun and, and I didn't play year round like they have all these select leagues nowadays. I played other sports and stuff like that. And nowadays I think kids get burnt out by the time they are in high school or there's not some type of shoulder injury. But I do owe my love for the game because of my dad."

"When I turned pro, it began to make sense because here I was competing against guys that were faster, stronger, more athletic, and in the minors, I was a million miles away from the big leagues. And I realized how awesome it was that my dad did make it to the big leagues. So I relied heavily on them because it's kind of cutthroat. You don't really know who to trust; coaches, players are so competitive that you have ulterior motives, jealousy, and stuff like that. So I relied heavily on my dad's advice. If I would struggle, he would be the first person that I would pick up the phone and, and not only just lean on him for some confidence, but to help me with my own self-doubts and my own feelings of do I measure up?"

All of which made Mark being called up to the major leagues all the more poignant. As Mark tells it, he was having an all-star year with the Mets' Triple-A affiliate. "My brother called me up and he told me that, you need to come home, dad's sick. So I caught a flight and I went home and I knew my dad was not going to survive. And so I said my goodbyes then because it was just a matter of time for the rest of his organs to deteriorate and fail. So I went back to Triple-A in pretty much of a numb state and [manager] Mike Cubbage calls me into his office and says, 'Congratulations, son, you're going to the big leagues.' I just was overwhelmed. He said I needed to join the team in San Diego. Tomorrow. The Mets will be in San Diego and you're going to be joining them there. I said, OK. So I caught the flight and I landed and I got to the airport and I called my mom and she said me hijo, which means my son in Spanish, you need to come home. Your father passed away this morning ... What was supposed to be the greatest day of my life was actually a triumph and a tragedy all in one."

But, as Mark noted, he will always have the memories of the talks they had after he became a professional. "When I started following his footsteps is when we started having conversations that I yearned for, conversations that we were on the same playing field. He was in the bigs but he was there and we could relate and we can discuss and talk about the game and I knew what he was talking about and he knew how I felt physically and emotionally and we connected and that was the bond that I'll always remember and hang onto because it was a short window. I signed professionally in 1981 and he passed in '87. So we had those years I would come home from a minor-league season and we would just talk and maybe have a few beers and just talk ball. It was great and those were actually the best years that we spent together when he was treating me like a man instead of, you know, one of the kids bothering him."

The Carreon family on street in Colton, Ca. named after Camilo. (Photo courtesy of Mark Carreon)

## THE MARK LEITERS

The Leiters are a pitching family: Mark Sr., a right-handed pitcher, spent 11 years in the major leagues with eight teams, compiling a record of 65–73 with an ERA of 4.57 and 892 strikeouts. Those accomplishments were overshadowed by brother Al, a left-handed pitcher who spent 19 years with four teams in the bigs, racking up a record of 162–132, a 3.80 ERA, and 1,974 strikeouts. Mark Jr.'s career is still emerging. A righty like his father, he spent 2017 with the Philadelphia Phillies, was claimed on waivers by the Toronto Blue Jays in late 2018, and in 2019, during spring training, suffered an arm injury that required Tommy John surgery. So far, his stat line is a W-L record of 3–7, a 5.53 ERA, and 106 strikeouts

Ask Mark Leiter Sr. about relationships, baseball, and his children, and he tells you about the son who made it to the major leagues and the one who we will never know if he would have.

Mark Sr. was with the Yankees in Ft. Lauderdale during spring training in 1991 when he received two pieces of news almost simultaneously: congratulations, you have a son, and good luck, you've been traded to the Tigers. There was a medical complication that resulted in Mark Jr. spending more than a week in the hospital. "I had to drive to Lakeland [where the Tigers trained]," Papa Mark said. "He ended up staying in intensive care for 10 days, all monitored up ... That was a tough thing. So he had a couple of days left in the hospital and I've been traded from the Yankees to the Tigers and I had to drive up to Lakeland. And then my wife came a couple days later with a brand-new baby."

But almost from the start, Mark Sr. and Mark Jr. bonded over baseball. "He loved it right away. I remember in the offseasons I would pitch him Nerf balls in the garage that I put some carpet down and stuff and he just loved hitting and all that."

Mark Jr.'s love of baseball was fed by a major-league environment, the ability to hang out in major-league locker rooms and play with other major leaguers' sons, especially when his dad was with the California Angels and the San Francisco Giants. "Kids were allowed in the locker room and out on the field at times, not during batting practice, but, then, with the Giants, he always loved coming to the field and playing with the other kids—

Matty Williams's son, Matty, Robby Thompson's kid, Mike Krukow's kid. They all played in the 49ers' locker room playing Wiffle ball, tape ball, or whatever. They were a good group of kids.

"He loved it. And I've talked to players whose kids never wanted to go to the field, so I didn't push it. He just loved it right from the start and I didn't need to push him. But as far as bonding, big time, big time growing up because I loved it when he came to the field. I would be disappointed when he didn't. "

Mark took an active role in his son's baseball development. Even when junior was only two years old, his father would pitch to him when they lived in an apartment when senior was with the Tigers and especially when they had a house with tennis courts when he was with the Angels.

"I'd go in there and pitch tennis balls, and every once in a while, he'd get ahold of one and hit the fence and for that young of an age to hit it again, like a massive bomb, you know, and he'd run the bases out," he said. "But it was always a lot of fun. And I never pushed him. I joke because, you know, people say, Oh, you push them in baseball. I'm like, no, when he was born, I put a brand-new baseball and a brand-new baseball glove and his crib. And that's all I did."

In playing catch with his son, Mark was passing on a ritual from generation to generation, although he was not as demanding as his father was with him and his brothers. "Playing catch with my dad was always fun because it's your dad and we were six boys in my family, so you didn't get a lot of time to play catch with your dad. But when we did, it was bittersweet with our dad because he was always about hitting your chest. If you threw it over his head, he'd make you run and go get it. So I guess we kind of learned, being pitchers, too, for that reason that when you throw to dad, better hit him in the chest with the ball because he isn't running down the street to go get it."

Early on, Mark Jr. let it be known that he wanted to follow in his father's spike steps. "What do you want to do for a work job?" Mark recalled his son being asked. He would respond, "I'm going to be a professional baseball player. Yeah, because that's all he really knew."

Mark Jr. knew early on he wanted to be a professional baseball player. (Photo courtesy of Mark Leiter)

Mark not only encouraged his son, he took an active role in his development, coaching him in Little League, always with an eye toward what would best prepare him for a professional career. "When he was a teenager, I took him out of a game one time. He had thrown only, like, 60 pitches, and he had a shutout going and he was so upset."

When asked by his son to explain, Mark said he responded, "You keep dropping your elbow and I tell you to raise your arm.

You think you're going to play pro ball if you blow your arm out in a seventh-grade game because you've got a shutout going? The fans were getting on me. Parents were saying, leave him in, he hasn't given up a run. I'm like, listen to these people. Like I don't know what I'm looking at? So my son, he didn't question me after that."

Mark continued offering his son advice, through the minor leagues and how to handle his first major-league game, once he got over the excitement of the call-up news. "The minute he told me he got called up, two minutes later we were back to business. What you need to do. So the only difference is the stadium's bigger. That's the only difference you're here because you're as good as major leaguers. You are now a major leaguer. So screw every batter that comes up. You're here too. And I had to let him know ... the most common mistake guys make is they get intimidated because it's the major leagues. You're not throwing to major leaguers, you're throwing to the catcher so don't worry about that. So, when he finally got into a game, my wife and I were watching here at home and he was at Dodger Stadium and it was terrifying. My heart was just coming through my chest and it was awesome because he did have a one-two-three inning and that was fantastic.

"If Mark didn't play baseball, we would be close, but we obviously wouldn't talk the way we talk now," Leiter said. "And we talk more the minute he gets to Florida [for spring training] than we do in the winter, because when he gets to spring training, we talk every night, every night. There's not a day that doesn't go by."

And they still play catch (at least until the Tommy John surgery), although now it is tied to Mark Jr.'s offseason training regimen to prepare for a baseball season and limited by the shoulder injury that is a holdover from Mark Sr.'s career.

Full circle for the Leiters in Philadelphia. (Photo courtesy of Mark Leiter)

Which brings us to the catch Mark Sr. never had but dreamt about. On Opening Day in 1994, Ryan Leiter, 10 months old, passed away from a childhood form of amyotrophic lateral sclerosis. And in talking about his relationship with Mark Jr., Leiter spoke about a dream he had a few nights previously. "I'm dying and seeing my son Ryan who passed away at 10 months old," he said, "and it was like Field of Dreams. And we were just playing catch in a grassy field. I don't recall, although I know it wasn't a stadium or anything, and it was just playing catch—the glove, the sound. My arm didn't hurt. It was beautiful. It felt real. It was awesome."

It was a reminder of how Ryan's death affected Leiter's outlook on life and how it shaped the way he dealt with his other children and their ambitions.

"I realized this, that this really sinks in when we go through this in life: A death, a very close death like that. We know when a friend dies or a grandparent, it's a part of life, but when you have a child that dies, you realize more than ever that forget tomorrow—the next hour's not guaranteed to us," he said.

"I changed a great deal after losing my son and so I would never discourage my sons or daughters from anything. My youngest, my nine year old wants to play in the WNBA, she loves basketball. All right, now let's go for it. Whenever she wants. If I need to go out and shoot baskets and dribble with her, we go out and do it. It's what she loves. So I wouldn't discourage them because life has had enough discouragement in itself, so if they're going to be discouraged, they can be discouraged down the road."

## MOOKIE AND PRESTON WILSON

There is a blood tie between Mookie and Preston Wilson and a father-son relationship, but not in the usual sense. Mookie Wilson was a New York Mets fan favorite even before he hit the ball that went through Bill Buckner's legs in Game Six of the 1986 World Series—an exciting ballplayer who could hit, steal a base, and play the field. He spent a decade with the Mets before finishing his career with the Toronto Blue Jays with a stat line of .274, 67 home runs, 438 runs batted in, and 327 stolen bases. Preston Wilson, born in 1974, was Mookie's nephew who, in 1978, became Mookie's stepson when Mookie married his brother's ex-wife and adopted Preston. Preston followed in his stepfather's spike steps when he was drafted by the Mets, came up through their farm system, and debuted for them in 1998 before being traded to the Florida Marlins two weeks later. Preston spent all or part of ten seasons in the majors, hitting .264 but amassing more home runs (189) and batting in more runs (668) than Mookie. Both have remained around the game in retirement, Mookie as a coach and Preston as a broadcaster.

Preston came late to baseball—he did not play until high school—which may seem odd, given the importance of baseball in the Wilson family and the fact that Mookie actually played on sandlot teams with his father.

"Baseball has been part of our family ever since I can remember," Mookie said. "Sandlot baseball, we called it. Games on weekends, Saturdays, and Sundays, and I was able to play on his team. ...It was one of the greatest things that happened to me in baseball and is something that every son should experience. It was a just a great, great feeling now to have something to share with your dad, and that's why it's so important ... It was actually one thing that I had hoped I would have gotten an opportunity to do with Preston: Imagine, if I could have played professional baseball on the same team with Preston, it would have been icing on the cake."

Unlike some ballplayers' sons, who know from the time they are very young that they want to follow on their father's footsteps, Preston did not exhibit any such interest even though he shared the experience of hanging around major-league clubhouses and making it onto the fields. And Mookie didn't exert any pressure.

"I pretty much let him make up his mind. That's one thing that I'd never done, try to push it in one direction or the other," Mookie said. "I remember him being in school here in New Jersey and he was pretty much a basketball player. That's what he did, he was a basketball player. And he just woke up one day, you know, I don't know where it came from. He just woke up and said he wanted to play baseball. And when he said that, my heart jumped. That's when we moved back to the Carolinas so he could play."

Once Preston made his decision, Mookie stayed interested but not overly involved—intentionally. "I tried to stay as far out of the coaching part of it until I was asked," Mookie said, "I never volunteered a lot because you could easily have a player in conflict between listening to his dad and listening to his coach, and I didn't want that. I wanted my input to be welcomed because the one thing I did pride myself on was baseball knowledge. But I, I didn't want to put my son in a situation, and I've seen it too many times, when there's a conflict between the parents and the coaches."

"I didn't see as many games in high school as I would have liked to have seen, but I saw enough of them, and it was great. My biggest thing was how quiet I remained on the sidelines while he was playing. I remember my father would always just pace. He would never say a word. He would pace near the fence outside. He will never say a word ... I know why he was walking somewhere because it was nerve-wracking. You know, it really is. You have to force yourself not to see anything because you don't want that attention. So I understood why he did that. So yeah, I've had that. I had strong feelings about that many times.

Not that Preston needed much coaching. "Preston was different. He was mature enough to understand and to know when he needed more help. He had sound baseball fundamentals, even in high school," Mookie said. "So there wasn't a whole lot that the coach could do really to change that. When he got to pro ball, it was a matter of repetition. I knew the coaches that he had. He had good coaches. But I was always there when he needed extra. I'm not saying that that was the ideal way to do it, but it worked."

"Baseball has always been a bonding thing in my family, with my dad, with my brothers and my sisters, as well, and with Preston, it's no different. It's a different bond, but it's just as strong a bond as anything. The one thing we have in common is the experience of playing minor-league baseball, playing for the same high school coach, and the same professional team. Nothing can replace that.

"It's a warm spot in my heart when I see a father and son playing catch in the ballpark and on the field, when I'm going to work. There's something warming about that and very right about that."

Mookie and Preston played for same High School coach. (Photo courtesy of Barry Colla Photography [Public domain])

# CHAPTER 3
## 246 (NOT A HEALTHY AVERAGE OR WEIGHT)

Having made the decision to go to Mets fantasy camp and having paid the considerable two-person fee, Mark and Josh were on a mission. A very simple mission.

To borrow from the famous advice of team owner Leon Hess in a 1995 Thanksgiving address to his then-winless New York Jets, "Now let's go out and show them we're not horse's asses."

After all, it's one thing to for a father and son to share a bonding experience that is happy, but quite another if what they share is the equivalent of a week in the dunk tank.

So both Mark and Josh knew that if they wanted to make the most of fantasy camp, if they wanted the photos and videos on Facebook be the one they posted themselves and not ones shared by acquaintances and strangers as candidates for a blooper reel, they needed to a) get in shape and b) clean the rust off their baseball skills.

Cue the music and start the montage. Start thinking about Sylvester Stallone as Rocky Balboa running up and down the Philadelphia museum steps as he prepares to fight Apollo Creed. Or Ralph Macchio as young Daniel learning how to wax on, wax off from Mr. Miyagi.

Mark back in the 80's channeling Rocky Balboa (Photo courtesy of Mark Rosenman)

Okay, the more appropriate analogies would be Tom Selleck as Jack Elliot in *Mr. Baseball* learning the way Japanese baseballers train, or Will Ferrell and Jon Heder learning the Iron Lotus in *Blades of Glory*. Or even Adam Sandler as Happy Gilmore stepping into the batting cage, batless, to sharpen his ability to block hockey pucks.

It wasn't going to be pretty, at least not at the start. But it had to be done. And it started with shedding pounds. Lots of them.

Over the years, Mark had been on many diets—thirteen by his count. He had been on diets named after people (Dr. Robert

Atkins, Jenny Craig); places (South Beach, the Mediterranean); and things (the Mayo Clinic). He had been on diets geared toward promoting lifestyle changes (Eating for Life) although the name does raise the question: who would ever eat for death? He had been on diets that ship food in plastic, microwaveable containers that make you feel like you are traveling economy class (Nutrisystem, Kettlebell Kitchen). He'd been on diets that use a shake as the basic staple, perfect for dieters without teeth (SlimFast), and ones that claim to use science to determine your individual regimen (the Blood Sugar Solution Diet, not quite as pleasant as Sherlock Holmes's seven percent solution). He'd consulted nutritionists and started a diet with the simple but effective name the Diet Center.

Strangely, Mark had never tried the single-food centric diets—the ones where you precede each meal by eating a grapefruit or cabbage soup, which purportedly fills you up.

Mark had lost count of the exact number of times he'd tried Weight Watchers. Three or four was his best guess.

Each time, Mark had lost weight. And each time, something had happened in his life to put the pounds back.

Most recently, Mark attributed his weight gain to the side effects of years of playing competitive sports—wear and tear on cartilage and bone from too many slides into bases and too many short stops and hip checks on skates. After years of suffering through bone-on-bone pain, Mark had a hip replaced, ending his competitive sports days and making him more sedentary. Suddenly, he wasn't working off that soft pretzel he'd buy on the way to the train home from work at night, or those dinners out with friends. And someone who weighed 195 as a varsity high school baseball player and 215 as an adult rec league softball and hockey player had gradually ballooned to 246.

Years of wear and tear playing Softball and Hockey led to Mark's Hip
replacement and subsequent weight gain (Photo courtesy of Mark Rosenman)

And 246, Mark knew, was a number not healthy for either a
batting average or a weight, and to get one 246 higher at fantasy
camp, he needed to get the other 246 down.

Mark decided to give Weight Watchers another shot.

Much had changed in the Weight Watchers program since
he had last Watched his Weight. Most notably, it was based not on
specific meals or foods, but on a point system in which each dieter
was assigned a daily allowed point value, and foods were assigned
points. Some foods were zero—white meat chicken, pickles, fresh
fruit—while some, understandably, were astronomical (a Burger
King Whopper is 21 points, almost a full day's complement; a
Dunkin' Donuts chocolate frosted donut is 12; a Pizza Hut personal
pan pizza is 20). The point is that you can eat what you want and
still lose weight if you stay within your daily points limit (Mark's

was 29). Want that Dairy Queen Blizzard (30 points, taking you into your overflow reserve)? Sure, but it's water for the rest of the day.

Keeping track of points is easy, and very 2019: through an app on a smartphone. A dieter can look up point values through the app and record it; to make things even easier, especially while shopping in the supermarket, a dieter can use the phone to scan an item's bar code to learn its point value and even save the results for future recording. The app also has stored the point values for most menu items at chain restaurants. Look up the restaurant, find the item and decide whether to order it or opt for the salad instead (minus the high-point dressing. Actually, one of the great surprises is the high point value for some of the salads at restaurants such as Applebee's).

Unchanged from the Weight Watchers structure are the weekly meetings. That's how Weight Watchers got its start: founder Jean Nidetch invited friends over to her house for coffee cake-less klatsches to trade diet tips, and a half-century later, the weekly meetings at studios around the world attract an estimated one million people to act as one multinational support group.

It's not quite Alcoholics (or Overeaters) Anonymous— no "My name is Mark and I'm fat ... Hello, Mark.."—and someone who joins Weight Watchers is officially on their own. No need for a sponsor; conversely, nobody to call at midnight when the gallon of rocky road in the fridge starts serenading you. But it is an opportunity to share milestone weight losses with a group, get nonjudgmental commiseration when you slip and get helpful tips. The company provides group leaders to channel the discussions, centered on a weekly topic provided by Weight Watchers central. The success of a group is partly measured by how well the group leader keeps the assembled focused, prevents a single individual from monopolizing the conversation, and promotes an atmosphere in which all group members feel welcome to contribute, even if they don't on a regular basis.

Mark looked at the different groups he could join – at different studios near his home, at different times, and with different compositions and decided to try the group that met on Sunday mornings in Huntington, New York. There was a men-only group that met at the same time a few miles away, but Mark opted instead for one that was co-educational and multi-generational.

The Sunday morning Huntington Weight Watchers group had men and women, seniors and high school students, husband-wife combinations, mothers and adult daughters, and mothers and high-school age sons. Some were just beginning their weight-loss journeys, others were well along to meet their goals. The group included first-time Weight Watchers and recidivists like Mark.

Mark signed up and weighed in. He was issued his official blue "Success Story" booklet, in which his weekly weigh-in would be recorded for his first 16 weeks of membership. Mark had never made it to his second booklet.

This time would be different.

It was different because Mark, essentially by luck, had stumbled into a group that clicked with him, one in which people came, and stayed, and after they strayed came back not just to Weight Watchers but to the Huntington 9 a.m. Sunday group. The people who came, and stayed, or returned, weren't just following the Weight Watchers program to retrain eating habits, they were perpetuating the method Jean Nidetch perfected with the weekly meeting among friends in her living room.

"I'm kind of the grandfather of the group because I've been coming here I think longer than most anybody" said Ed Nitkewicz, a lawyer and local school board member who had been coming to the Sunday morning meeting on and off for a decade. "I try to stay here because of the family environment we have."

Nitkewicz, who is well short of grandfather age, gained weight intentionally as a college football player but realized after graduation that unless he lost that weight, he would not even live to the age of his father, who passed away at 52. "I have a son with autism, he's an only child," Nitkewicz said. "He's going to be living in a group home some day and the only normal or regular lifestyle he is going to have will be as long as he can have some family around him....I wanted very much to live as long as I can, so my motivation was my son."

To Nitkewicz, Weight Watchers "was like a lifestyle program rather than a diet ... I needed something that I could do long-term. There was a period of time after I hit lifetime [the goal weight that results in weekly fees being waived] when I stopped coming to the room and I fell right off the ladder."

Back he went to the meetings. "It was the accountability that I feel during the week, the accountability that this room gives me. So when I reached for that extra candy bar or if I reach for a cake, it's this moment in time, and I think about it."

Lauren Grasso joined the group for family reasons, too: her high school age son, Joseph, who joined her in the program. Grasso had tried Weight Watchers before, lost weight and gained it back. "It was always on my mind about losing weight, trying to be better, more healthy, for myself, for my kids," she said. "But when I mentioned Weight Watchers, he looked up at me, I'll never forget, at the kitchen table and said, 'Mom, maybe that's something we could do together.' That was it. That was the defining moment that there was no going backwards because my kid was asking me in some shape or way that he needed help. So we came the next day."

Over the course of the little their time together at Weight Watchers, Lauren lost 113 pounds and Joseph, 62. "I think of how both of us have done, I think that perhaps if he wasn't here with me, I might not have made the goal. I think that he keeps me in check. If I have a donut, it's a green light for him. So what parent would want to set a bad example? So I can't have the donut because I don't want him to do it," she said.

Like Mark, one of the keys to success this time was also finding the right group. "I think the meetings are very important, which in in the past, I started to go and then it was like, I don't need to go anymore," Grasso said. "I know everybody always says about this group—I think it's this group. I think it's this Sunday, this group, the people here. I don't feel embarrassed to say, if I failed or succeeded or whatever it is. The group, it's almost like a little family."

Part of it, both Nitkewicz and Grasso said, was due to the skill of the leader, Lisa LaRusso, who keeps the discussion going and engages the whole room. "Lisa is wonderful in letting the group find its voice in the room," Nitkewicz said. He remembers giving her advice when she took over the group, having been through five leader transitions over the decade he has been a member. "I remember saying to Lisa, the hardest part that you're going to go through is this: You're going to want so badly to do most of the talking in the room, and the idea with this particular group is that this group has a voice. It is a lot of leaders in the room."

Lisa's success, Nitkewicz said, was due to "her ability to grow into the role to let a very strong group of people who have been together for a long time, at least many of us, to allow their voice to be heard . . . the reason this room stands is because somebody like Lisa has the confidence in your own skin to let others co-lead with her."

Grasso put it more simply: "For me and Joseph, she for me is like a sister maybe that I'd never had. I feel very comfortable with her. I don't trust many people, but I feel like I trust her. I really love her and my kid loves her and we have been here over the summer when she was away on vacation and, and Joseph said, 'Lisa's not here, we're not here.'"

Everyone in the room, it seemed, evolved into roles. Grasso was the one with the recipes. Nitkewicz was the one with the institutional memory and a quick quip. Others shared weekly stories about their personal lives, and how eating played a role in their work routine. They would talk about successes and failures, and about the stresses that took them away from their path and resulted in weight gain.

Measured successes were large and small: the young man who joined with his wife and lost 200 pounds with her at his side, long after she had gained lifetime status for herself; the man who considered a victory when he reduced his pizza consumption to a couple of slices from eating an entire pie.

Mark became one of the leaders. He always had stories to share, working baseball and hockey into his narratives and well as his food quirks that he had overcome (like the soft pretzel on the way home from work). He related in considerable in incredible detail his adventures on his newly acquired Peloton exercise bicycle. People listened and laughed. For the first time, he made it to his second 16-week book.

"What I've seen in Mark is just exactly what I've seen in some of the most successful stories in this room," Nitkewicz said. "Somebody has come in, not just dedicated to the weight loss but dedicated to sharing that journey with other people ... It reminds me of me from 10 years ago because I watched somebody during the journey narrate their journey and then inspires so many other people in the room. When you are able to speak with courage and conviction about your failures and your successes, you're touching people in this room who don't have that kind of voice."

Mark's path wasn't linear. There were weeks when he gained and explained to the group why. There were weeks when his loss was not as great as he hoped. But over the long run, the pounds came off, and from March 1, 2018 to January 20, 2019, his weight dropped so that when he went off to fantasy camp, he was all the way down to 217.

The Sunday Morning Huntington Weight Watchers class, a very special and inspiring group of people (Photo courtesy of Mark Rosenman)

As for Josh? "The biggest challenge in getting ready for fantasy camp was managing my weight," he said.

As was chronicled earlier in this book, weight issues had plagued him practically his entire life—remember how he surmised his weight kept him from making the junior high school baseball team? —and losing weight had also provided motivational challenges. As an adult, he was doing well, generally, until his activity was slowed by knee problems and the issues resulted in weight gain. Even before the prospect of fantasy camp, Josh began taking steps to lower his weight, including surgery. But fantasy camp provided yet another spur to bring his weight even further under control.

His vehicle was the ketogenic diet, an ultra-low-carbohydrate diet (similar to Atkins) that eliminates carbs and replaces them with fats. The goal is to get the body into a metabolic state called ketosis, in which the body breaks down fat for energy. No groups, no meetings, just individual willpower. Over the two-year period preceding fantasy camp, Josh dropped 75 pounds, including 25 in the four months leading up to camp.

Of course, losing weight was only half of the lets-not-embarrass-ourselves initiative. The other half was getting in shape and reawakening their baseball skills.

Mark took the lead here, signing them both up for weekly (and sometimes twice weekly) sessions at a Hicksville, New York, business, G&L Baseball Plus, that bills itself as having "Long Island's premier batting cages." The facility is somewhat reminiscent of Play Ball, the indoor fields where Josh played and Mark coached the Little League Cougars, with entrance to the workout area through the pro shop and lighting-challenged cages, pitching mounds, and an infield practice field that does little to hide its converted warehouse aura. An eclectic mix of banners line the walls—from Pepsi-Cola and Budweiser to Fox News to Ford and Toyota to teams that have trained there.

Running them through their paces was someone who also had a multigenerational baseball tie. His name was Reggie Jackson, and his familial relationship was not to the Hall of Fame slugger, but to his father, Al, an original New York Met. Al Jackson was a mainstay of the fledgling (and terrible) 1962 Mets' rotation whose 20 losses that year proved how good a pitcher he was and how bad was the team behind him. As Roger Craig, the ace of that staff and another 20-game loser, noted, it takes a really good pitcher to get enough starts to lose that many games. After ending his playing career, Al Jackson spent decades as a pitching coach at both the major- and minor-league levels, most of those years in the Mets' system.

A pitcher like his father (although right-handed while Al was a southpaw), Reggie tried to make it in the Mets' farm system but never advanced past Double A. He spent time as a scout for the Mets, as a minor-league coach and as Hofstra University's coach before becoming a youth baseball instructor and trainer.

Two Aces Reggie and Al Jackson (Photo courtesy of Reggie Jackson)

Mark had discovered Jackson not through his Mets team contacts, but from two longtime Mets fantasy campers, Ed Kavanagh and Gary Pincus, who in addition to providing a reference, joined Mark and Josh in the workouts.

Jackson would run them through the whole gamut of baseball. He pitched to them. He hit grounders to them. Some of his other students pitched to them. Occasionally, he would let Josh switch hit. And as the months wore on, he would add simulated games to the sessions, breaking them into teams and starting each batter with a 2-2 count and doing game situational hitting. Jackson determined what was a hit or an out.

For Josh, the workouts were as much a reminder of his needed conditioning as they were a chance to sharpen baseball skills. "The running was the hardest part," he said. "It showed me just how out of shape I still was."

But he also was concerned about the knee problems he developed years earlier, which he attributed to his weight. "Working through that was always in the back of my mind," he said. "You go in with the mindset that you're not going to overdo it, then once you start playing the games, all of that goes out the window and you are unable to hold yourself back from things like diving for balls or trying to run full speed." So increased flexibility was an imperative.

Mark had a broader agenda that encompassed all phases of his game. He needed to work on his footwork, as well moving to his left and right, so he could play his natural position, third base.

Mark and Josh working on footwork. (Photo courtesy of Mark Rosenman)

Mark also needed to overcome some of the effects of his hip replacement, especially at the plate. "Since the hip replacement, I still cannot generate the torque from my lower body, so I was all hands. My eyes were still good, as I could still get to most pitches, but clearly, I had issues with changeups and curves."

The Peloton exercise bicycle Mark purchased about halfway through the training process helped with his conditioning, especially in terms on stretching his hamstrings to add flexibility.

Like any training regimen, there were days and there were days. "Some days I hit like a beast, others were brutal," he said. All in all, I came away happy with my increased endurance and felt okay but not great about my hitting."

But was four months of two-a-weeks of reawakening dormant skills enough to avoid embarrassment in front of Josh's work colleagues and the former major leaguers Mark had cultivated as friends? Would struggles to lose weight increase speed and stamina to allow them to go from first to third on a cleanly fielded single? Would they endure the rigors of two games a day under the almost-hot January Florida sun?

They were about to learn. The preparation was over. Cue the music for the end of the montage. For better or worse, it was time to play ball.

# CHAPTER 4
## YOU CAN'T SPELL FANDOM WITHOUT D-N-A

Is fandom nature or nurture? Do we devote our lives to rooting for a particular team because it is ingrained in the biological fabric of who we are, or because someone close to us, from a very young age, inculcated in us the imperative of being a die-hard fan of a specific team and at the same time learning the necessity of hating the opposition?

People may say, for example, that they "bleed Dodger blue," but if you look deeply at their genetic structure, you won't find anything in their genes and chromosomes to produce that hematology. And as much as Mark Rosenman would tell people being a New York Mets fan was is in his DNA, it's not there. And he knows. He looked.

Mark's 23 and Me composition report came back with the results that he was 96.2 percent Ashkenazi Jewish, 0.7 percent

Broadly Southern European, 3.0 percent broadly European and less than 0.1 percent Native American (which may help locate the lost 10 tribes of Israel but does nothing to explain his fandom). There is no "M" gene that would cause him to bleed Mets orange and blue.

To explain his devotion to the baseball team from Flushing, you need to look instead to a particular individual: his father, Morris Rosenman. He was an original Mets fan, picking up from his loyalty to the New York Giants, a loyalty broken when the Giants moved to San Francisco in 1958. What did not travel out to the West Coast with them, for Mark's father and for many other Giants and Dodgers fans also wounded by the westward migration of their team, was hatred for the New York Yankees and, by extension, anything American League.

So Mark's father became a Mets fan and, when he felt Mark was old enough—eight, to be exact—he decided it was time to ingrain Mets fandom in him. So, as fathers across the country and across time do and have done, he began Mark's passage into fandom by taking him to a game.

Mark remembers it vividly. It was Friday, August 30, 1968, and of you look it up, you will find that 34,425 people attended the game, Art Shamsky hit a fifth inning grand slam and second-year phenom Tom Seaver pitched a masterful three-hitter, striking out 11 en route to an 8–2 Mets win over the St. Louis Cardinals.

What the box scores and game recaps won't show you is all that Morris Rosenman did to hook Mark on his beloved Mets: the souvenirs he bought Mark (a yearbook, a scorecard, an autographed team ball, a Jerry Koosman button). And the box scores and game recaps do not quantify the value of the conversations about the game, the ballpark experience, the comments about the other fans and how to watch a game in person rather than on television. Nor does the printed word capture his passion or his pride in seeing his only son absorb the lesson and become hooked himself.

Ticket stub and souvenirs from Mark's first game. (Photo courtesy of Mark Rosenman)

That night, Morris Rosenman created a lifelong Mets fan. While memories of the game are hazy, and Mark's recollection had to be refreshed by research, Mark's memories of him and how he related to him that day have not faded.

So when the time came, Mark knew exactly what he had to do to continue the generational string and pass his Mets fanaticism on to Josh. And he started considerably earlier than Morris Rosenman did with Mark.

Josh's age was measured not in years, but months when he attended his first baseball game—not the Mets, but the Red Sox at Fenway Park—and it had an eventful interruption. Mark and Beth were visiting Beth's brother, and he had gotten tickets for all of them. They drove straight to the ballpark from Long Island.

New papa Mark was convinced Josh was ready for baseball. "From a very early age, he was always very alert and always looking at everything," Mark said. Only once they got to the game, something seemed wrong with Josh. "He threw up, and Beth said he felt a little warm," Mark recalled. "She felt something wasn't right because he was very lethargic." Things got worse as the game went on, and they decided to leave early and take Josh straight to Massachusetts General Hospital, where Beth's brother, an ophthalmologist, had an affiliation. Doctors decided to take a spinal tap, which confirmed a diagnosis of meningitis. "So the first game we went to is not a fond memory because we then spent 10 days in the hospital, and for a while, it was touch and go," Mark said.

Three months later, Josh would attend his first Mets game, against the St. Louis Cardinals. "In retrospect, it's idiotic, there's no question," Mark admitted. "We had season tickets to the Mets. That's really the only reason we went. I was going with my friends at the time and Beth had not been to a game, so it was a night out. Instead of getting a babysitter, we took him. He has zero recollection of that whatsoever."

Josh's first Met game.(Photo courtesy of Mark Rosenman)

The first game Josh probably remembers? Mark thinks it may be a Mayor's Trophy Game (an annual Mets-Yankees charity game that died out when interleague play began and the two teams started playing for real) when Josh was three. Or it could be one in which Josh's entire Little League team went to the game and the team's name was mentioned on the scoreboard.

Josh does not remember the details of the game—like Mark, memories are hazy, even if the number of elapsed years is smaller—but there are facts that demarcate the beginning of a lifelong fandom (and eventually, for Josh, a job). Josh especially remembers the neon–light players that adorned the exterior of Shea Stadium and the general demeanor of the crowd, especially at the end of the game. "I remember how when you left the game, you would walk down those ramps with everyone chanting, 'Let's Go Mets!' It felt almost as if the place was shaking ... I always thought it was pretty amazing to have an entire stadium chanting the same thing. Or do the wave. I remember thinking, *How do all these people know what to say or do at the same time?*"

As for souvenirs, he remembers buying packs of baseball cards of Mets players and mini-bats that had players' names on them. Edgardo Alfonzo was his favorite.

Josh's Mets fandom would carry him through high school and college, so much so that when he was looking for summer internship, he obtained one with the Mets' New York-Penn League farm team, the Brooklyn Cyclones, which would, a few years later, lead to him being hired by the big club.

Shea Stadium was gone by then, but Josh flashed back to his youth every time he showed up for work at Citi Field. "My entire first year at Citi Field, I remembered when I came as a fan. It didn't feel normal until around my third year that this was just another day at the ballpark ... and seeing the old apple in the parking lot [that used to pop up when a home run was hit] always reminded me of Shea."

The Apple reminds Josh of his trips to Shea every day he goes to work (Photo courtesy of U.S. Customs and Border Protection [Public domain])

Mark's and Josh's experiences are not unique. Baseball fandom crosses ethnic, economic, and even gender lines. But common to all is the frequency with which the child learned about baseball from the father—not only the basics of the game, but which team to call their own. The vehicle for this transmission could take many forms: attending a game, watching a game on television together or listening on the radio, a phone call to discuss the previous night's action. Sometimes, but not always, instruction on how to play the game or a parent's fandom for a child's Little League, high school, or college team fed the relationship.

Ronnie Spector, a Rock and Roll Hall of Fame inductee and lead singer of the 1960s group the Ronettes, remembered, "My father was a [Brooklyn] Dodgers nut, and if he wanted to go to the game, he has to take little Ronnie—he used to call me Butchie—and from the time I was five years old until the time I was eight or nine, I went with my father. It was Ebbets Field, and my father would buy me a hat, turn it to the side, and say, 'Butchie, sing.' Buy me some peanuts and Cracker Jack ... and my father, and all the people around me at the game at Ebbets Field would applaud me. And I would do all this stuff, and my father loved it, and of course, I loved it, and I loved that he loved for me to sing, so it all fit."

Ronnie Spector's public singer career may have started at Ebbets Field.
(Photo Courtesy of GAC-General Artists Corporation-management [Public domain])

In her memoir, *Wait Until Next Year*, historian Doris Kearns Goodwin writes about how her father taught her how to score a baseball game and how she would listen to Dodgers games on the radio, fill in her scorebook, and wait until father came home from work to go over the game's activity "There was mastery as well as pleasure in our nightly ritual," she wrote. "Through my knowledge, I commanded my father's undivided attention, the sign of his love."

Twenty years later, baseball would still play a role in their relationship: she wrote that during the Mets' 1969 championship run, she and her father would discuss the day's events daily. "It almost seemed as if, through the medium of baseball, we could recreate the old intensities," Goodwin wrote. And after her father passed away three years later—while watching a Mets game on television—she married and "began to raise a family of my own, finding myself reenacting many of the rituals I has shared with my father."

Politicians, entertainers, writers, astronauts, actors—the vocation makes no difference. Dedicated baseball fans either picked up their enthusiasm from a parent or eagerly looked forward to transmitting it to their children. And as could be expected, those who went into the business of broadcasting have fond memories of how their fathers shaped their commitment to the sport and their decision to make it their life's work.

This is how people from different walks of life detailed their path to fandom:

## THE VICE PRESIDENT: DAN QUAYLE

James Danforth (Dan) Quayle served two terms in the House of Representatives and eight years in the U.S. Senate, representing his native Indiana, before becoming George H. W. Bush's running mate in 1988 and being elected the 44th vice president of the United States. After leaving office in 1993, Quayle eventually settled in Arizona, where he spent much of his childhood while his father ran a branch of the family's newspaper publishing empire, and has worked as an investment banker and as chairman of the Global Investments division of Cerberus Capital Management, a multi-billion-dollar private equity firm.

In 1990, Quayle was elected to the Peter J. McGovern Little League Hall of Excellence in Williamsport, Pennsylvania. The museum honors former Little League players who "have demonstrated a commitment to excellence in their chosen profession and exemplify the values learned as children in Little League."

Vice President Dan Quayle was huge White Sox fan.

(Photo courtesy of George Bush Presidential Library and Museum [Public domain])

Of course, Quayle's father, James Cline Quayle, played a large role in instilling those values, both on and off the Little League field.

Starting, of course, with which team the family rooted for. "My dad was a huge Chicago White Sox fan," the former vice president said. "And so therefore, the whole family grew up to be Chicago White Sox fans. .It was something he had a love for. He really did. And we went to games with him and everything. So it was important to him."

Quayle remembers what may have been his first game, driving to Chicago from Huntington, Indiana (where his father was running the newspaper), to Chicago to see the White Sox play. He was either six or seven years old. "The White Sox had Minnie Minoso and Nellie Fox, Chico Carrasquel, all those great guys. But they never won a pennant because the Yankees, the Cleveland Indians, and the Detroit Tigers were always much, much better," he said.

An important part of shaping the bond with his father was listening to White Sox games on the radio. "We didn't have much TV in those days. We listened to the games at night and my dad taught me how to keep score. I would keep score listening to the radio late at night or sometimes on the weekends."

As for Little League, the former vice president first played on a team sponsored by the Huntington *Herald Press*, where his father was the general manager, and in Arizona, where the family moved when he was eight and where his father served as an assistant coach.

"I was always the leadoff batter because I was short, I'd walk 90 percent of the time, I'd always get on base ... I always played second base and the thing is, I was a pretty good fielder. I wasn't a very good hitter, but I'd get on base and be able to score runs."

Eventually, he turned to other sports, most notably golf, which led to him playing on the DePauw University golf team. But his love for baseball continued, and he passed that on to his children (two sons and a daughter)—although they did not inherit his love for the team that plays on Chicago's South Side. Instead, they developed an affinity for the team closest to where they were living: the nation's capital.

"They grew up Baltimore Orioles fans because Washington didn't have the Nationals then, they just had the Orioles and it wasn't that far a drive," Quayle said. "So we'd drive up and watch the Orioles play ... I took them to a couple of World Series games."

And now, living in Arizona, Quayle gets to pass his love of baseball onto another generation: his grandchildren. He takes his grandsons and granddaughters to baseball games, just like his father took him, with one major difference: "When I went with my dad, we'd sit way out in left field, about row 29. You could barely see the park. We've graduated. I can get some really good tickets, Ken Kendrick, the owner of the Diamondbacks, is a really good friend, so I buy some tickets from him and they're good. So I look at them, and I go, you guys are really spoiled. I sat in the bleachers and here you are, you know, right behind home plate or right behind the first base dugout.

"So they have it a little differently. I'm trying to teach them how to keep score, because I think that's important and how they can do it get every strike so you know exactly what happened, which you can do. It just takes some time to do that."

Going to a game, he noted, is "just a special time to spend with your dad, your sons, and now your grandsons and granddaughters. When you go to the park and you sing the songs in the seventh inning and stand up for the national anthem before the game begins. It's all about America: the American sport, baseball."

Not to mention that baseball crosses political lines as well as generational ones.

"When I first met [former President Barack] Obama was at the inauguration, his inauguration, so it was at this lunch they have after he's inaugurated and we're chatting. I said, 'We've got a couple things in common.' He said, "What's that? I said, 'Well, you're the 44th president. I was the 44th vice president,' and he goes, 'Oh, okay.' And I said, 'You're a Chicago White Sox fan, and I'm a Chicago White Sox fan. And he goes, 'Well, that's really cool.'"

## THE SONGWRITER: DAN BERN

Baseball has played a prominent role in Dan Bern's career. The guitarist, painter, novelist, and singer has written more than 1,000 songs, a considerable number of them about baseball, including 18 collected in an album, *Doubleheader*, released in 2012. He also produces short music videos of his works, 10 of which are on his website, www.danbern.com. Of those, three are baseball-related, including one, "The Legend of Yasiel Puig," that features his daughter, Lulu (the reason for which he describes below).

What may be somewhat unusual is that Bern's evident love for baseball and knowledge of the game is self-taught. His father, he noted, emigrated from Lithuania at the age of 40, and never picked up the sport.

"His relationship with baseball is absolutely zero," Bern said. "I remember sitting with him once, watching a game, and we must have sat there for a good hour and then he turned to me and said: 'Why is there hitting and running like that?'

"So I had to find it myself. I found it initially through books because we didn't have a team ... I sort of found it in a literary way and then broadcasters and then onto the games myself ... When I found it, it was kind of like my connection. I think one of my first connections to real American things and the American lore. That was sort of my way in. But as far as my dad, I got a lot from him, but baseball was not something that I got from him."

Bern did not see his first major-league game until just after he graduated from high school, when he went on an Amtrak trip with his best friend and stopped at Dodger Stadium for a Dodgers-Giants game and bought seats in the outfield. The Giants won, "which made me happy because at the time I was a Giants fan," he said. "I saw [Willie] McCovey play late in the game. I think he'd come back after his stint with the Padres. I also remember watching the outfielders throw warmups to each other. I'd never see a ball go that far, that straight."

If you're looking for backup for the phrase *impressionable youth*, you can look no further than young Dan Bern: the baseball lore that molded his love for the game helped form his worldview and became the basis for some of his songs. "Those stories are so powerful, and especially when I was a kid, but even beyond that, but when you're a kid, and that's what you're reading, you just take a lot of life lessons from those things and those, all those characters in those stories are just bigger than life.

"Baseball just is woven through everything. I didn't intend to make a baseball record until we did it. But those songs were already written. It wasn't like I need to write a baseball song. They were just the next song that I wrote, and it happened to be with baseball woven through it. I think that's why, in my opinion, that they're good songs."

The titles help tell the story: "The Golden Voice of Vin Scully," "Come Back Andy Pettitte," "Johnny Sylvester Comes Back to Visit the Babe" (about the hospital bedridden boy for whom Babe Ruth promised to hit a home run), "When My Buckner Moment Comes," "The Sun Shines Over McCovey Cove," and "42," to name a few.

A more recent song is the one about Yasiel Puig, inspired by Bern's relationship with his daughter, Lulu, who is nine. "She's developed a real interest and kind of passion for the game, of playing it and the lore of it and going to the games."

It started when Lulu was barely a year old.

"We were living literally an eight-minute walk to Dodger Stadium," Bern said. "So we just went a lot. Part of what has drawn me in the last few years to being a really strong Dodger fan and Puig fan was that right when her sort of awareness was really becoming strong about who was down there on the field was right when Puig came along and he was so much fun. So it was really a way for both of us."

"We went to Game Four of the [2018] World Series down in LA and it was unbelievably emotional because we're there and Puig hit a three-run homer and it was the day after that 18-inning game and it was the most excited I've ever been in a ballpark. And we were all, I think, to the point of tears. And then literally 15 minutes later it all came unraveling and you know, the whole ballpark was yelling at the manager to not make the bonehead moves we saw him about to make, which he had made. And you know, so it was, it was pretty emotional. And then Puig gets traded a couple months later."

Lulu also plays softball and her father has tried to help out as best as his travel schedule allows. And father and daughter do share the joys of having a catch, cementing their bond.

"I think it all adds up, you know what I mean?" he said. "Just today we went out in the street and we had a catch. I think it's a really strong and deep thing. I never had that with my dad. I'm assuming that because I do have it with my daughter, it's part of what will keep us bonded and close."

Baseball keeps Dan and Lulu close. (Photo courtesy of Dan Bern)

## THE COMEDY WRITER: ALAN ZWEIBEL

Alan Zweibel is what they call in baseball a five-tool player as he is one of the most versatile comedy writers and satirists of our time. Zweibel was one of the original *Saturday Night Live* writers, creating some of its more memorable sketches and characters; he co-created and produced *It's Gary Shandling's Show*, and wrote for shows such as *Monk* and *Curb Your Enthusiasm*. He has written screenplays and best-selling novels.

Two of his writing efforts look at the relationship between fathers and sons and have baseball elements: *700 Sundays*, which he co-wrote with Billy Crystal, and *Happy*, essentially a sketch about a baseball that reconnected a man with his father years after they became estranged.

The one-man show *700 Sundays* looks into the relationship between Crystal and his father, and includes one Sunday in which Crystal and his father attended a Yankees game that spawned the comedian's lifelong passion for the team. Zweibel has said that *Happy* is partially based on the baseball part of his relationship with his father.

"The earliest recollection of anything with my dad baseball-wise was in the street in front of our house," Zweibel said, "him throwing, I would say was usually a, Spaldeen [the street vernacular for the pink rubber balls manufactured by Spalding], and he would throw it up real high, and that's how I practiced catching fly balls. Most often I wore my mitt even though it was only a rubber ball. So I would practice catching with one hand, with the glove hand, and go further and further away and then the long throw back to him. I marveled how high he could throw."

Zweibel remembers the first game he went to with his father – at Yankee Stadium in 1960 in which the Chicago White Sox beat the Yankees, 5–3 with Ralph Terry relieving Whitey Ford on the mound for the Yankees and future Met Bob Shaw hurling for the ChiSox. But embedded more deeply in Zweibel's memory is the second game they attended, the next year, 1961, also at Yankee Stadium, what he called the "magical year." And the memory wasn't just about what happened on the field.

"That was the Maris-Mantle home run thing, right?" Zweibel said, "September 1, 1961. They played the Tigers and they won, 1–0. With that lineup they had—six guys hit better than 20 home runs if you count Johnny Blanchard—and, this was a one-nothing game ... It was not a slugfest by any means, you know, but I think that Frank Lary, the Yankee killer, pitched.

"I have a very, very vivid recollection of that game, and I almost count that as the first game we went to, though technically it was the second one. It was just so cool. Here's why I'm laughing: It was also the first day that I ever had Chinese food in my life. We grew up kosher. I went to work with my dad. And then before we went up to the stadium—he worked in the city and was a jeweler— he took me out for Chinese food and then told me not to tell my mother. So that's emblazoned in my brain."

Zweibel went on to see the original Mets play at the Polo Grounds in 1962 and continued his Mets fandom when they moved to Shea Stadium in 1964. "I'd go with my dad, and when I got older, I'd go with my friends. The impression that I had looking around and seeing fathers and sons—as a young boy, 11, 12, 13, I knew that I wanted to be a father. I knew that I wanted to someday be able to bring my son to a baseball game."

Fast forward a number of years. Zweibel marries and his first child is a son, Adam. And he wastes no time in inculcating his love for baseball in Adam. "It was the summer of '82 and we have footage of this, we videotaped it. We had rented a house in Malibu —I had writing projects out in LA and so we lived there for the summer. So Adam wasn't even a year old. We have footage of me playing roly polies sitting on the grass and if I really look at it, there's no way he was playing catch, but rolling it . . . But I counted it as our first catch, to me that was a milestone."

Zweibel couldn't wait to take Adam to games, playing on his contacts to get really good seats, including Rusty Staub, Keith Hernandez, Mets front office executive Thornton Geary (the son-in-law of legendary *Daily News* columnist Dick Young) and actor Len Cariou (known then for Broadway but more recently for his role on the long-running television series *Blue Bloods*).

"We used to hang out at Rusty's restaurant on 73rd and third in Manhattan, and a lot of the Mets would come there and it was very, very exciting," Zweibel said. "When I took Adam to games with us, we got really good seats because of the people that I knew. Once we were in the press box. And I was showing Adam, I was telling him, what the play is, and this and that. And then they had this new young player. I said, his name is Darryl Strawberry. And I remember Adam crying saying that I was teasing him because nobody had a name like Strawberry, what's his real name?"

Adam was a player— he would eventually play college baseball—and Alan was an involved father from the start. "I became the commissioner of the Little League and we almost had to move because parents get pissed off at me because, God forbid there was a rainout, I would reschedule. You can't have the makeup game on the same day that a little Joey Levy had a Bar

Mitzvah to go to and he was the best shortstop. Robin and I would walk into a restaurant and see people and we'd turn around and go somewhere else."

"Our Saturdays were spent watching him play, or he and I would be alone at the field letting him pitch to me," Zweibel said. "So the roles were reversed." He and wife Robin would pack their other kids into their car and follow Adam to high school tournaments in Arizona and northern California. "It became a family ritual," he said. So much so that even after Adam graduated from college, having spent four frustrating years riding the bench on the Michigan baseball team, he signed up for what Alan described as a "Sunday sort of semi-pro league," Alan and Robin Zweibel would still go to their son's games. "And he was 24 at this point," Alan said.

Eventually, Adam would marry and have a son, Zachary. Grandpa Alan said, "Zachary is 10 years old and a very good ballplayer. Reminds me of Adam when he was little. I go to all the games as a grandfather. Adam not only goes to all the games as a father, but I can see how he works out with him in the backyard, which was reminiscent of the same way I worked out with him and the same way my father worked out with me."

This passing of the baseball torch also created a dilemma for Papa Alan. "It was such a rite of passage, that when our grandson was ready to go to his first game, I had a leading thought of taking him. I censored myself—no, no, no. That's a father-son thing. ...It was such a right, of passage that, you know, it should be a father and a son."

"I have been to baseball games with Adam and his son Zachary, you know, unless you can take them to the first game, like I said, I didn't want to impose, but plus they didn't invite me, so I didn't go. ...We went, I want to say two years ago. My literary agent married George Steinbrenner's granddaughter. So he got us into Steinbrenner's box at Yankee Stadium. We watched this particular game from the owner's box. And it was really cool because we got a picture of Adam, his son, Zachary, and Mariano Rivera.

Three generations of Zweibels love baseball.(Photo courtesy of Alan Zweibel)

"It's weird, but if I felt that my son wasn't paying enough attention to the baseball part of the relationship, I'd feel the need to step in and pick up the slack a little bit. But from everything I've observed, the kid's more than covered."

For Zweibel, the memories he has of sharing baseball with his father are vivid, even if they are not as much for his father. "Years later, I mentioned to my father that September 1, 1961. He didn't remember it. He didn't have the recall of it and it really bothered me. It bothered me that it wasn't the milestone for him as it was to me.

"I made it a point to Adam, and to Zachary ... to remember. Not only everything I remember, but I kept scorecards, just so I would have a piece of memorabilia from the experience that I would give to him to let him give to his son."

## THE ASTRONAUT: TERRY VIRTS

Terry Virts spent 16 years with the National Aeronautics and Space Administration, where he participated in two space flights: a two-week mission on the Space Shuttle Endeavor in 2010 and a 200-day flight in 2014-2015, an assignment that included piloting the Space Shuttle, commanding the International Space Station, three spacewalks, and performing scientific experiments, all while working closely with multiple international partners. Virts flew with and led Russian Space Agency cosmonauts during some of the tensest relations with Russia since the Cold War.

A photography buff, he took more than 319,000 photos in space, the most of any space mission. His images are part of an IMAX film, *A Beautiful Planet*. But while in space, Virts had another photographic goal: to capture the images of all 28 cities with a major-league baseball stadium, an homage to the fact that baseball is his favorite sport. Virts also took a replica Jackie Robinson jersey and a Baltimore Orioles jersey with him in orbit.

'I love photography and I did lots of other stuff, but baseball is just my thing and it's American and I wanted to reach out in a way that would be culturally important," Virts said. "I mean the space stuff, amongst the space nerds, everybody knows what's going on, you know, that small segment of the population follows everything about space, but most Americans don't ... So I thought that would be a way to kind of cross a bridge into a segment of the population that might not know anything about space. So I did that. It was my idea and we just tried to have some fun on Twitter. It was pretty good and some of the teams would retweet it and put the pictures up on the screen in the seventh inning."

"I became a fan as a kid," Virts said about his childhood growing up in Maryland. "I don't remember my first instance with baseball, but I know it was because of my dad. He took me to Memorial Stadium when I was a kid and I saw Brooks and Frank Robinson play there at Memorial Stadium. Going to the ballpark when I was a kid was a really unique thing. I mean it was like once a year or something. And so for whatever that's worth I guess thats the way I got introduced to it through my dad taking me to see Orioles games."

As Virts describes it, his father is the personification of a lifelong fan. "He's like 75 and he still wears a really cheesy Orioles cap. He folds it so that it looks just ridiculous, but he thinks it's cool. And yeah, he wears that Orioles hat around. My grandfather was, too. He died a few years ago, but his nursing home was like a shrine to me and to the orioles. He had about 5,000 pictures of me in his room and about 100 Orioles hats. ...He used to tell me he was a plumber, like a steamfitter. He put boilers and heating systems in buildings, and he did that at Memorial Stadium, apparently, when they were building it... I never saw him go to a game or anything, but I guess as a younger man he did. But when he got older, he never went. But he was always a fan."

In passing the torch from grandfather to father to son, each picked up his own facet that they particularly loved. For Terry Virts, it was statistics. "I'm a baseball savant. I must be annoying to go to a game because I'm just talking all the time about all the details." Not so his father. "He remembered the guys from when he was young, and I have no idea who these guys were on the Orioles from the fifties and sixties. So he would talk about them. The one thing I can remember about my dad: Every time they brought a reliever he would just go, 'Oh God, here we go.'

"And he's like the king of the anecdote, right? Like a reliever gives up a run and of course the manager should have left the starter in and you know, relievers are terrible and blah, blah, blah, blah, blah. And he never understood the reasons for that. So it was just funny to hear him complaining about bringing in relievers and to this day, he's still an Orioles fan and he said now he can watch it on his Ipad or whatever because they have all these plans. So I'll get a text from him: here we go again. Every time that comes in during a game, the conversations, it was either a) about the old guys from the fifties and sixties or b) he was always mad when they brought a reliever in."

Virts does not have many memories of playing—by his own admission, he regrettably was not that skilled—but he does remember one day a piano recital conflicted with his Little League championship game. His mother made him go to the recital. When it was over, they sped to the field, arriving just as the game ended. The upshot? "I never played piano again," he said. But while his playing days ended, his fandom continued to grow. He attended the

1979 World Series, in which the Pittsburgh Pirates came back from a 3–1 deficit to beat the Orioles. For the 1983 World Series, in which Virts's Orioles defeated the Philadelphia Phillies, 4–1, he sold hot dogs so he could go to the games.

It was more difficult to follow his favorite team while serving in the military—he was stationed in Korea and Germany and was at the mercy of Armed Forces Network Television, which was a single channel that presented a variety of programming —"one sporting event per day, one soap opera per day, and a movie and one sitcom. So it was very rare that we saw any baseball, much less the Orioles."

Returning stateside and joining NASA in Houston gave Virts a chance to see baseball again—and to become friends with Astros management—as well as coach his son from T-ball through Little League. "A significant part of my life for a decade was coaching baseball," Virts said.

But then, Virts's career got in the way. "I went into this long-duration training when I was gone half literally half the year in Russia and Japan and stuff. And then I was in space for 200 days. So kind of after Little League, my intense involvement in that stuff ended. And when he got to high school, I really wanted to actively again make a conscious decision to not be his coach. Like I just wanted him to go be his own man. Because if dad's there, I don't know, there's pluses and minuses to that ... I wanted him to go learn how to deal with coaches who are jerks and whenever. Unfortunately, we had a really bad baseball coach at the high school and we had a great football coach at the high school. My son quit baseball actually while I was in space. ... And that broke my heart because baseball was his best sport ... So he's probably going to make more money as a doctor or an engineer than as a baseball player."

Coaching his son was a significant part of Terry's life. (Photo courtesy of Terry Virts)

But, Virts noted, baseball remains "the glue that holds us together. You know, men don't talk. We don't have emotions, whatever, but we can always talk about baseball. And with my grandfather and my dad and my son, it's like a completely common thread that we have. Without it, I don't know what we would talk about. There are real issues about relationships that are really important. At the end of the day, baseball is not important. It's just a game. But it's like the means to an end to build those relationships.

"I've heard it said that girls relate in circles and men relate in lines. Like the girls would rather sit around a table and talk to each other and men would rather sit on the bench watching the game and kind of talk out of the side of our mouth, and that's what you do at a baseball game. You sit there, you don't have to look at each other, you watch the game, but you can talk the whole time. And I think it's a great way for men, fathers and sons, to build and cultivate and maintain a relationship."

## THE ACTOR: CHAZZ PALMINTERI

Over a lengthy and distinguished acting career, Chazz Palminteri has played gangsters (*Analyze This*), gangsters who want to be writers (*Bullets Over Broadway*), law enforcement chasing gangsters (*The Usual Suspects*) and a host of other characters. But his career has largely been defined by a semi-autobiographical story he wrote, *A Bronx Tale*, that started as a one-man show, became a film directed by Robert De Niro in which De Niro plays the main character's father and a Broadway musical. Palminteri still performs the one-man version.

Baseball plays an important part in the relationship between the protagonist, young Calogero (Palminteri's real first name) and his bus driver father, Lorenzo. How true to life was the story?

"My dad took me to Yankee Stadium when I was very young. My father was a die-hard fan – and my mother. My mother was as bad as my father as far as die-hard goes," Palminteri said. "My mother passed away at 97. She was still saying, how'd the

Yankees do? That was pretty amazing. My father passed away at 90 and you know, they always said we're going to watch the Yankees today. So they were die-hard Yankees fans and they got me to be a die-hard Yankees fan.

"My fondest memory is the first time he took me there. I must've been six or seven I guess, and him taking me through the tunnel and then seeing the field, how huge, and you see the green grass and how huge everything looked. ...I spoke to a lot of kids about that and that's usually their memory too, seeing the tunnel, going through it and then seeing the green grass. And I just grew up loving Mantle and Maris.

"My dad was a Joe DiMaggio fan, but I was too young for that. But he would take me to games, and we would watch the games on television. When he was driving the bus, he would listen to it on the radio and I would sit behind him. So, wow, I would say that my dad and my mother were the biggest influence on my life as far as being a fan goes.

"People say the sport is dying a little bit and I really believe that it's so expensive now that a lot of these parents can't take their kids any more. And, and I think that hurts it because I think the way you become a fan is through your parents, that's how you do it. ...Like I did with my children the same thing, you know."

Also evocative of art imitating life is Palminteri's memory of his first catch with his father—at City Island, the end of the line for his father's bus route both in real life and in fiction. "It was City Island, and my earliest memory, I would bring my glove and a ball, and at the very end, it was the last stop, and he had time before the next bus went out. So we'd hang out there, and sometimes, he'd take out the gloves and the ball and we'd play catch."

Palminteri has two children—a son, Dante, and a daughter, Gabriella. Both are die-hard Yankees fans and they get to go to around 10 games a year. "It's a thing, I can't explain it. It's a love of the game of love of that's your team, especially us. We were born in the Bronx, right? You go up to Yankee Stadium, Wow. That was pretty great."

Chazz and Dante share a moment at the old Yankee Stadium (Photo courtesy of Chazz Palminteri)

And when he does go to games, he has an unusual routine, an homage to when he went to games with his father. "We didn't have a lot of money, so we didn't have the best seats. We would sit in the upper deck in the very last row and all the way one on the top a lot of times, you know, and I remember that. So now I go to the games that I sit behind the dugout, or behind third base or behind first base. And when I do, I know a lot of the players and the players give me a ball or two sometimes.

"So what I do is I look around and I sign the ball. I signed my name on it. Sometimes I wait until I go upstairs and me and my son did it this last time and we go up the elevator, we go to the top deck and then we go to the last row in the top deck. I mean, you couldn't get any higher up. And I see if I see a father and a son. And the last time I went, last week, I had two balls to give to two different people, but I saw this father with two sons, one on each side of him and they were dressed in Yankee uniforms and they in the last row of the highest deck. And I walked over to them and they look at me. I said, 'Hi.' And I said, you know, my dad used to take me here and we used to sit all the way up here. And I remember how exciting it was and it brought back a lot of memories. I said, I want to give these to your sons. And I gave them each a ball and it was like I gave them like a $100,000 each."

## THE BROADCASTERS' WING: BOB COSTAS, HOWIE ROSE, AND CHIP CARAY

Why do people decide to become sports broadcasters? Do they need to be rabid fans of a certain sport as a prerequisite for broadcasting them? Is there anything different in the growth of their fandom that could predict their career choices? How much of that do they owe to their parents?

Bob Costas, Howie Rose, and Chip Caray are all distinguished sports broadcasters. Each of the three has broadcast multiple sports. But each has also made most of their reputation calling major-league baseball on television and radio.

Costas has the most varied background of the three. He has called boxing, NASCAR, professional basketball and hockey, hosted an NFL studio show, and anchored NBC's Olympics coverage. But baseball is his longest and most abiding love, calling games first for NBC (and hosting studio shows), then on ESPN's twice-weekly telecasts, and currently for MLB Network.

In some circles, Rose is best known for an iconic hockey call of a game-winning goal in the New York Rangers' 1994 run to the Stanley Cup —"Matteau! Matteau! Mateau!"—and he spent years as the New York Islanders' television play-by-play announcer. But his longest stint has been doing play-by-play for the New York Mets, the team he rooted for as a youth. Rose has been in Mets broadcast booth since 1995, emcees the on-field pregame ceremonies, and is regarded an expert on the team's history.

If anyone had tried to predict Caray's future occupation as a child, baseball broadcaster would have been first on the list. After all, his's father, Skip, and grandfather, the legendary Harry Caray (Chip's given name is Harry Christopher Caray III), were both longtime baseball play-by-play announcers. In fact, Chip, a year out of college, was hired to work alongside his grandfather on Cubs games; when Harry passed away before the season started, Chip took his place. After seven seasons, he went on to TBS to work Atlanta Braves games with his father. Early in 2009, he hooked on with FOX Sports South, doing play-by-play for Braves games.

Here's what they had to say about their fandoms:

## BOB COSTAS

How did Bob Costas become introduced to baseball? "Almost by osmosis," he said. "If anybody introduced me to it was my father because he was following the games, like millions of other dads in that era. And those games were either on the radio or on black and white TV. And my earliest recollections of it is maybe when I'm five or six years old. Not specific, just kind of the, the idea of the sound of the game or the look of the game being on television, which is so different than it is today. No center-field camera. Every shot was from high home. But that's when I first remember it and then beginning when I was seven or eight, I can begin to remember specifics."

Likewise, Costas doesn't remember the specifics of the first games he attended with his father, although he does remember the year, the place and the possible reason. "He took me to one game at Ebbets Field and one game at the Polo Grounds in 1957, the last year that the Giants and Dodgers were in New York. I don't know if he had some sense that It was going to be the last year; he just took me to those games. All I remember about Ebbets Field is kind of the atmospherics of it. And the only thing I remember specifically about the game at the Polo Grounds was we were seated so far away and I was sitting up on his shoulders, but he pointed out Willie Mays to me standing in center field. He said, 'See that guy? No, no, not that one. The one in the middle. That's Willie Mays. He's the best player,' and that's the only thing I remember about that game.

"The game that I remember specifics of as the first one I went to [was at] Yankee Stadium which was 1959. I was seven and the Yankees played the Orioles late in the season and I remember that Mantle was not in the lineup. He was hurt and the Orioles won the game, 7–2. but Johnny Blanchard hit a home run for the Yankees."

Costas became a Yankees fan, with a special appreciation for Mickey Mantle (he would eventually deliver the eulogy at Mantle's funeral). His father's team allegiance shifted regularly. "He was a gambler, so the team he liked was the team he'd bet on that day," Costas said. But as an accommodation to his son, John Costas, an electrical engineer by trade, would refrain from betting on the Yankees' opponent if they were going to a game, "so that the visits to the ballpark wouldn't be completely ruined or weird. But there were times when just during the season he'd have bets against the Yankees. And if the Yankees won, I would have to cheer silently in my head."

Costas became a student of the game. "I learned because I was a big Yankees fan, I knew all the other important players in the American league. And then when the Mets came into existence in 1962, when I was 10 years old, I would always watch the Yankees first. If the Yankees weren't on, I'd watch the Mets and I learned the players in the National League that way. And then I started playing Strat-O-Matic with some friends of mine in the neighborhood and Strat-O-Matic taught you not only about current players, but they had an Oldtimers edition, and you learned the lineup of the '27 Yankees, the '34 Gas House Gang [St. Louis Cardinals] or the '54 Giants or something like that. So that actually helped in some rudimentary way with understanding of baseball history. And then I would sit and watch these games or listen to these games with my dad."

Costas remembers having catches with his father and participating in another rite of baseball passage: learning how to break in a glove. "The first glove that I got, despite the fact that Mickey Mantle was my favorite player, was a Rocky Colavito model glove. And the way all kids broke the glove ... My dad showed me this, what you do, you put that oil on the glove and then you put a baseball in the pocket and you tie a rubber band around it because that stiff feeling that the glove has when it's new made you believe, as if when you were seven, you were somehow Luis Aparicio or something, you could feel everything. You're lucky if you could catch something that was underhanded, right to you from 10 feet, but still, with the glove being too stiff, you felt like you couldn't handle anything. So the sooner it loosened up, the better you felt about it and the more you felt like a big leaguer. So yeah, we played catch on the front lawn."

Bob's dad John taught him how to break in his glove..(Photo courtesy of Jeffrey Beall [CC BY 3.0 (https://creativecommons.org/licenses/by/3.0)])

How did his father know the correct procedure? "There was no YouTube, there was no television, there was no radio and people still knew how to fix a wagon wheel. They knew how to put a saddle on a horse. People just learn how to do stuff."

Bob Costas played Little League and John Costas would go to the games, critiquing his son's performance. And Bob would pass his love of baseball on to his children, son Keith and daughter Taylor; both, in fact, got to work with their father—Taylor won an Emmy  as an associate producer for NBC's Olympics coverage and Keith as an associate producer of MLB Network's *MLB Tonight*.

Did his father's love for baseball result in Keith also making the sport his life's work? "You think of the millions and millions of kids who love baseball, love whatever sport they love and their parents have no direct connection to it," Costas said. "They're doctors, lawyers, attorneys, whatever, you know. So, it isn't automatically a nurture thing. But he was around baseball and I was taking him to baseball games, also to NBA games, too, because NBC had the NBA but mostly baseball games, not just games that I did, but Cardinals games in St. Louis. We would go to a couple of dozen games a year and just hang around."

When his children were little, Costas said, "We had a place in Florida, that we would vacation in February and March and I would take them to spring training games with me. So he was always around the game and he was always asking questions and I taught him to read a box score when he was six years old and, you know, that kind of thing.

"Now he's an associate producer at the Major League Baseball network. He's in my ear from the truck when I'm calling a game, offering thoughts and observations and little tidbits and whatnot, and he produces segments that, that I'm part of. So there really has almost never been a time since he was old enough to understand what baseball was when he and I did not have an ongoing baseball conversation and connection."

## HOWIE ROSE

Howie Rose attributes his love for baseball entirely to his father. "He really gave the game to me," Rose said. "When I was seven years old, we were still living in the Bronx and he started taking me to Yankee games and I just fell in love with everything. The surroundings, I mean the atmosphere, the enormity of the ballpark, the beauty of the ballpark. But like most seven-year-old boys, I just got hooked on baseball. I couldn't even tell you why. I just did. My first hero was Roger Maris and the happiest, bar none, times of my youth were sitting in the ballpark next to my dad."

Howie's dad Bob "gave the game" to him.(Photo courtesy of Howie Rose)

"I'm trying not to romanticize the game because it's personal for me," he said. "I don't need to dig deep to try to understand. It's a visceral reaction that when I was in the ballpark with my dad watching baseball, it was really the confluence of a lot of different things. It's the obvious: spending time with your dad; being someplace you like; learning the game from him and being awed when I go to an Old-Timers Day at age seven or age eight. And usually it was Mel Allen who was the emcee and he would start to introduce the players and it was like a little game: How quickly into the introduction would my father know who the player was? I mean, for me it was a game I played. How fast is he going to get this? And those things stay with you because ultimately, they transcend baseball."

Rose's memories are tinged with some sadness about what might have been. "My dad has been gone a long time," he said. "He had Alzheimer's, really before anybody ever heard of Alzheimer's. So even though he died when I was 24, I really lost him when I was like 17, 18, so I never knew him as an adult. I didn't have the privilege of having a fully matured relationship with my father because it was always very much father-son and the son was still, despite however rebellious we are at that age, subservient. So I certainly missed out on that and maybe that's why I treasure the memories I had at the ballpark so much because they're basically all I have. But the excitement that I got in those early days, just learning the game, it was all encompassing. It was. I was in a vacuum that included nothing but baseball."

Rose said he is reminded of his father every time he is near Yankee Stadium, and even when he sees a photo of the old ballpark and its neighborhood. "I saw a picture of Yankee Stadium that they said was taken in 1962 from up the street. Maybe it was Babe Ruth Plaza or the street. Could have been 157th Street, something like that, but my grandparents, my dad's parents, lived right across the Concourse from the Stadium on Sheridan Avenue. And then later on, my aunt, my uncle, and my cousin moved to a building directly across the street from the stadium on Girard Avenue ... My dad loved to dress [up] and he'd always want to stop into a clothing store. I could hear Bob Sheppard starting to announce the starting lineups and I'd be trying to pull him by the neck out of that store. I saw this picture on Twitter yesterday, and they said it was from 1962 when I was eight years old. How the stadium looked back then from the perspective of walking down that street with my dad. That just should send chills down my back."

"He didn't go to me with me to Shea Stadium much. I guess when I was 12, I started going to games without parental supervision. So it was different. The Mets were kind of mine and the Yankees were his and we shared them a little while, but anytime I'm around Yankee Stadium I get incredible flashbacks. "

Rose did remember one Shea game with his father, against the Chicago Cubs during their improbable 1969 pennant run. The Mets won. "He liked that. I'm not sure, but it might've been the last game I ever went to with him, but I just got such a kick out of him enjoying it. And it would have been like the following week probably we went to the Bronx, to my aunt and uncle's house for Rosh Hashanah and the whole family was together, a whole father's side of the family was there and he was a well-known Yankee die-hard who used to make fun of me for rooting for the Mets. And I remember that at some point during dinner, my dad, as a throwaway line knowing what was going to happen just said, 'How do you like my Mets?' And in unison there must have been eight people that yelled: 'Your Mets?'"

The Bronx—his maternal grandparents' apartment, to be exact —was the site of Rose's fondest baseball memory. "My dad was between jobs in the early sixties, well '61, and we lived with my mom's parents and there were just so many rooms in the house. I had a brother and sister and so this is September of 1961 and I've got to go to school the next day when the game started at 8:00 back then. And the deal I had with my dad was, since he didn't have free reign of the house either, it wasn't our house, we had a portable

TV in the room I slept in and he would come in. We'd watch the game together until whatever the time was I had to go to sleep and he would order me that he was going to turn the sound down on the TV and I had to turn around and face the wall and not watch the TV, close my eyes, and go to bed because I had to get up for school.

"Well, you know how that works and every five minutes and I picked my head up and turn around and turn around, turn around and finally, I fell asleep. Well, now Maris hits 57 or 58, whatever it was. My father sees the home run and I could still remember their flashing the number on the screen. He literally shook me out of a sound sleep and said, look, look, look, Maris just hit number 58. So that's the one that always sticks out because that's the cement right there. That's, you know, that's where you inherit the passion with something like that."

## CHIP CARAY

You would think that someone who went into the same profession as their father and their grandfather would have started at an early age, sitting on the lap of dad or grandpa and learning, as it were, at the feet of the masters. But that was not the case with Chip Caray, which argues for a genetic predisposition to broadcast more than an environmental one.

"My parents were divorced when I was seven years old. My grandparents were divorced before I was born and so, as I've told many people before, I never really knew my dad until I was a high schooler or an adult," Caray said. "He was in Atlanta. I lived in St Louis, which is where I grew up. ...Most of my formative years with my dad, were like fans at home. I would watch on TV. And somehow instinctively I just knew from the tone of his voice whether he was having a good day or if the Braves were playing well or if he's having fun or if he'd been out too late the night before."

"Fortunately for me, with the way my career path has turned as an adult, once I had my own children and I was doing basketball games in my 20s, he and I got to connect through professional sports, not just baseball but basketball, and more so in Atlanta when I came there in '91and began to work with him on a part-time basis. And more so in '04 when I came back from the Cubs. It's really an interesting thing to not have this super-duper close bond with your father as a 10, 11, 12-year-old kid."

So it is all the more interesting the relationship had with Skip Caray helped propel him into following in his father's line of work, noting a particular game where he hung out with his father at the office.

"I knew I wanted to be a broadcaster when I was in high school," he said. "The Braves were playing the Dodgers, so it's '82 or '83, a great pennant race with Tommy Lasorda's Dodgers and Joe Torre's Braves. Dad was doing a game on WSB Radio ... I was home for the summer, so it might have been August before school was starting. Bob Watson came off the bench, hit a pinch-hit home run off Steve Howe. Fulton County Stadium goes nuts. You couldn't get out of there. So we sat around for an hour, and I'm listening to Vin Scully and Ross Porter and my dad and Pete [Van Wieren] and Ernie [Johnson] tell war stories around the table, and back in the days when they treated you like an adult and you can have a cocktail after the game and nobody freaks out because the lawyers get involved. And it's midnight and I never, I'll never forget this. It's midnight. We're driving home in my dad's powder blue, four-door Volvo and the station announcer comes on the air and says, it's midnight, Atlanta, and the time chime goes on the air....

"Seventy-two degrees. Last night the Braves beat the Dodgers, eight-seven. Here's Skip Caray's call. And they played my dad's call on the radio. And all of us in our lives have an ethereal moment where something happens and you, whether it's you see the woman you're going to marry, or you know where you want to live, or a song sticks in your head. They played my dad's call and the hair on the back of my neck stood up and I said that was awesome. He said, what are you talking about? I said, someday I want to do that, and we lived about 10, 12 miles from the ballpark and dad didn't say a word. We finally get home about 12:30, had a bite to eat. He brought himself a cocktail. I was having a glass of water or something and he said, 'Were you serious about what you said in the car?' And I said, 'Yeah, I am. And he said, 'Okay, we start tomorrow.'

"Never once did my dad push me into the business. Unlike his dad. Harry kind of tricked him into becoming a broadcaster. I had a very influential maternal grandfather who is a successful dentist in St. Louis for 50 years and was kind of like a surrogate dad to me. I thought about going to medical school and then, when I got to college, I thought about going to law school, but this is where my heart is. It's what I love doing. I guess it's what I was born to do. Whether it's family or not, it's just I have a connection to be able to describe what I see and not script too many words."

So, as Caray noted, his relationship with his father became close, even if they missed out on Chip's formative years. "The point of the game is to come home, right? Score a run and come home," he said. "I think for my dad and me personally, the two of us were able to come home and come to a safe and happy place where we were really content and, and loving of each other, especially in the last years of my dad's life. And I'm forever grateful for that opportunity. That was the whole point of me going to Chicago when I got the Cubs job. I was supposed to work with my grandfather until he decided he didn't want to do it anymore. And, unfortunately, he passed away the spring before I started working there. And so that was a big, giant open loop that our family never got to close.

"Baseball for me has brought, brought me and my father full circle. I got to be his son, take him to the doctor, get him his medicine, go to lunch with him, pick up his bags on the road, trips, help him off the bus, get them a drink on the plane. He got to know my children and his grandchildren as a result of baseball and our closeness and our familiarity.

Baseball brought Chip Caray "home".(Photo courtesy of Preston Mesarvey [CC BY-SA 2.0 (https://creativecommons.org/licenses/by-sa/2.0)])

"And the fact that three of us were able to broadcast at the same time in the major leagues was really cool. Something that I appreciate now more than then because I was just starting out and young and dumb and naive and didn't understand who Harry Caray was and what he meant to the city of Chicago and didn't really fully understand what my dad meant to Atlanta. So I find out all those things firsthand.

"I have three boys and a girl, and I have a Harry the fourth and he wants to broadcast, believe it or not ... And he's got a talent. He is kind of interested in what dad does. It's really funny looking at that through the lens as the older person now because I see some of the same confidences and insecurities that I had at the same time. And like I've said to my wife, my kids are all much better looking than I am. They're all hell of a lot smarter than I am because of her side of the gene pool. But I have no doubt in my mind that if it's something they want to do then there'll be great at it. But, and again, whatever success they had won't be because of me. It'll be because they're good people and that's the most important thing."

# CHAPTER 5

## PLUNKING JOE PEPITONE

Randy Hundley spent 14 years in the major leagues. He was an unspectacular hitter known primarily for his defense and his leadership, especially as the workhorse catcher on some very good Chicago Cubs teams in the late 1960s and early 1970s (as well as brief stints with the San Francisco Giants, Minnesota Twins and San Diego Padres). In 1968, he caught an amazing 160 games.

As injuries took their toll, Hundley began paving the way for his post-baseball life (he retired after the 1977 season). He worked for a small insurance company. He obtained his broker's license and got a job in investment banking.

And then in the summer of 1982, Hundley was running a baseball camp for children at a college in Palatine, Illinois, when he had lunch with a restaurant entrepreneur named Rich Melman. Melman's company, Lettuce Entertain You Enterprises, has been responsible for the concept of over 100 restaurants across the

United States. According to a 1992 *Chicago Tribune* story, Melman told Hundley at the lunch that he had a cousin in Los Angeles with a concept of his own: a baseball camp for adults.

The light bulb went on in Hundley's head. And baseball fantasy camps were born.

Hundley ran the first Cubs fantasy camp—what is regarded as the first-ever baseball fantasy camp—in 1983, and it was such a success that he quit his investment banking job and started running camps full-time.

Hundley would not stop at one camp. Other major-league teams hired him to run their fantasy camps, too—the crosstown White Sox, the St. Louis Cardinals, the (then) California Angels to name three. Over the years, he has cut back his schedule and now only runs the Cubs camp. At the age of 77, Hundley is still going strong.

Randy Hundley started the first Fantasy Camp in 1983(Photo courtesy of Jewel Tea via tradingcarddb.com [Public domain])

"As a kid, I always dreamed of being a big-league ballplayer, I mean like when I was two years old," Hundley says in promotional video on the Cubs Fantasy Camp website. "When I had the opportunity to play in the big leagues, I thought everybody should have the opportunity to see what it's like to be a big-league ballplayer. So that's how it all started, way back in 1982, and here we are thirty-some-odd years later still doing the camps."

In his video sales pitch, Hundley says, "What's so unusual about the camp is that you experience the same thing as a big-league ballplayer, and that was my goal initially, and that is one we have been able to uphold, and I'm very proud of that."

Actually, experiencing the same thing as a big-league ballplayer is not that unusual. It is the proclaimed selling point for all of the major-league fantasy camps, whether it is the Cubs, Tigers, Reds, Orioles, Yankees, Mets, or any of the other teams that run fantasy camps—and that is almost all of them. The differences among them relate to how they recreate the major- league experience—playing night games, for example, or having batting practice in the major—league ballpark (in the dead of winter, as part of the training preparation), or the number of "kangaroo courts" or how the fines from those courts are appropriated (they can give the proceeds to charity; at least one uses it as the tips for the clubhouse staff).

A major selling point teams use is the opportunity to rub elbows with some of their former major-league heroes, whether it be on the field as the manager of their teams, at lunch or dinner, or even, as one team highlights on its website, in the hot tub at the hotel, which seems a markedly friendlier setting than that the whirlpool in the trainer's room. Another major-league team, the Cardinals, offers the opportunity not only to be coached by a former major leaguer, but to play with two of them on your team.

All are cashing on a phenomenon that transcends baseball, or all sport, for that matter, and relies on the truism that we all want to be something other than what we are, fed by the unattainable real-life answer to the question, "What if?" Add to that the increasing amount of disposable income available for travel and a growing propensity for different, immersive vacation experiences, and you have the ingredients for a burgeoning industry whose poster child is the fictional character Walter Mitty.

An indication of this circumstance's prominence is that it has been the subject of studies in a peer-reviewed scientific publication called *The Sport Journal* (an interesting concept itself: a scientific journal dedicated to sport), which has given it a name —Sports Experience Tourism, of which fantasy camps are a subset. A 2012 article, titled "Sports Fantasy Camps: Offering Fans a More Immersive Experience," explored the attraction of fantasy camps to fans and the potential benefits for the clubs.

"Sports fantasy camps are used by sport organizations for a number of reasons," the article noted, "including (a) creating more brand loyalty; (b) generating additional revenue; c) getting involved in philanthropic ventures; (d) providing additional sponsorship opportunities; and (e) stimulating sport tourism in the local economy."

Indeed, the fantasy industry has come a long way since the late 1970s, when each week, Herve Villechaize, as the trusted assistant Tattoo, would shout, "Ze plane!" to alert his boss Mr. Roarke (Ricardo Montalban) to the arrival of the week's crop of fantasy seekers on their television-series island. Fantasy has become a billion-dollar industry—a 2011 article in the publication *Smart Money* estimated it as $3 billion to $5 billion annually—and it encompasses more than just sports. For the right fee, fans can indulge their fantasy to live like a rock musician, an astronaut, a survivalist, a special ops agent, or a Hollywood star.

Fantasy Island may have inspired an entire fantasy business. (Photo courtesy of ABC Television [Public domain])

The fantasy camp experience has made it into our pop culture—in a 1993 episode of the classic sitcom *Seinfeld*, character Kramer talks about arriving home days early from a New York Yankees fantasy camp that was curtailed by an incident that began when he inadvertently punched Yankee legend Mickey Mantle in the mouth during a brawl. Kramer spurred the brawl when, while pitching, he not-so-inadvertently brushed back former Yankees first baseman Joe Pepitone. "Joe Pepitone or not, I own the inside of that plate," Kramer said, describing how he knocked Pepi down, only to see him continue to crowd the plate. "I had to plunk him," he said.

"Joe Pepitone or not, I own the inside of that plate" (Photo courtesy of Mark Rosal [CC BY-SA 2.0 (https://creativecommons.org/licenses/by-sa/2.0)])

More recently, in 2017, Mets fantasy camp was part of the plot line for two consecutive episodes of the sitcom *Kevin Can Wait*. In the first, the main character, Kevin Gable (Kevin James) needs to lose weight and get his cholesterol down so he can go to the fantasy camp. In the next episode, he faces the dilemma of going to fantasy camp or coming out of retirement and working on an important fraud case (he misses the camp).

The same year, Red Sox fantasy camp formed the basis for an episode of the animated sitcom *Family Guy*. Main character Peter Griffin wins a church raffle in which the prize is a week at the camp, at Fenway Park. He takes his wife, Lois, along and she ends up not only playing but being better than him. The script captures the essence of fantasy camp as Peter describes getting a hit:

"I ran like a champion that day, pushing through the pain of two torn hamstrings and a ruptured groin to leg out the hit at Fenway Park I had always dreamed of. But nobody noticed, because the account manager from B of A who was playing third base had a massive coronary trying to field my crappy little nubber."

As sports go, baseball may be the sport that best lends itself to the fantasy experience. Certainly, there is a greater preponderance of over-50 beer league softball players than over-50 basketballers or footballers. Baseball, with its historic reverence for history, also lends itself to events that celebrate past performances and past performers, which help explains the proliferation of baseball fantasy camps.

Of the 30 major league teams, 24 held 22 fantasy camps in 2019. Most are run by the teams themselves. Exceptions were the joint fantasy camps offered to fans of the Dodgers and White Sox; the joint one offered to Athletics and Mariners fans; the Giants camp and Hundley's Cubs camp.

At least two teams—the Reds and the Indians—offer their fans the opportunity to feel good about themselves while feeling bad because of their injuries by using proceeds to benefit the team's Hall of Fame and Museum (the Reds) or the team's charities (the Indians), making a portion of the fee tax deductible (consult your financial advisor).

Fees range from a low of $3,550 (Tigers) to a high of $6,950 (Cardinals). Most offer similar attractions and amenities, and the cost difference among teams may be attributed the number of hotel nights, dinners, or the type of accommodations. Upgrades are available, typically for a single room. But for an extra $1,300, the private operator-run Mariners-Athletics camp sells a VIP package that includes round trip airfare, a single room, a custom bat, a private one-on-one baseball clinic, and golf with the major leaguers (to replicate the off-day experience, especially for Yoenis Cespedes fans).

Typically, teams offer discounts to repeat customers, although some temper the benefit by requiring the campers to reuse their old uniforms. Lower-cost packages are also available for those who want to partake of the camaraderie without playing; the Phillies segment that to an extreme by offering both a Phan package at their Phantasy camp (bring your spouse, significant other, agent, publicist, personal trainer or anyone else in your entourage) and a General Manager package, which lets you rub elbows with Phillies front office personnel and witness the player draft.

The teams usually offer either a single one-week session or two, with no differentiation between the weeks. Most are held in late January, just before the start of spring training, although a couple run in November and the Tigers run a weekend mini-camp in August at Comerica Field in Detroit (obviously, when the big-league team in on a road trip).

The Yankees scheduled three different 2019 camps: a "traditional one," one for women only, and a Family Fantasy clinic for parents/children or grandparents/grandchildren. Held over three nights in November, the team calls the clinic a "unique adult and child bonding experience at a premier baseball facility [the team's Tampa spring training complex], hosted by the most storied franchise in sports history."

Among fantasy camps, the LADABC Fantasy Camp stands alone in that it was both privately operated and unsanctioned. But it is as much a testimonial to allure of the experience, and the addictive nature for those who have participated, as the ones run by the major-league clubs.

The camp traces its roots to a team-run camp at Dodgertown in Vero Beach, Florida, that existed for many years until the Los Angeles team packed up its spring training operation and moved to Scottsdale, Arizona, after 2008. With its new Arizona complex, the team decided to stop running fantasy camps, which left a void in the lives of Dodgers fantasy camp regulars. "Veteran campers would still get together at various reunion events and spring training," said Mark Stone, owner of the LADABC Fantasy Camp. "After a couple of years with no camps, when we saw our friends, all we heard were grumblings that the new ownership was doing nothing to keep the camp tradition going. So we decided to try to do it ourselves. It was not done with the intent to make money but rather to preserve the tradition we had known for almost 30 years."

The LADABC camp is a privately operated and unsanctioned camp (Photo courtesy of Mark Stone)

In 2011, about 100 campers gathered and ran a camp in Vero Beach—arranging with Major League Baseball to use team uniforms and signing up former Dodgers as coaches. They ran camps again in 2014 and 2015, while continuing what proved to be unsuccessful negotiations with the Dodgers for sanctioning. And then, in 2016, the Dodgers resumed running their own camp. But the LADABC camp continues.

Stone contends that his camp provided a closer camper-former major leaguer experience than the team-sponsored camps because, in his words, it is "overstaffed to ensure that many of the past coaches could participate. We did this because it was important to the camp veterans and not necessarily to the Dodgers organization." Additionally, he notes that because his camp provides all meals, campers get to spend more time with their former heroes and receive more personal instruction.

"We've had nothing but positive feedback from the coaches because the experience has been very much like they used to have back at Dodgertown," Stone said.

Does it work as a business model? According to Stone, "We'd love to make a profit, and hope to break even, but thus far it's been a loss. So what we get is intangible. The same fan experience, playing ball under the tutelage of the former Dodger greats and the camaraderie we've developed with former campers."

At the camps the minimum age ranges from 30, the limit at most of the camps, to 25 and even down to 21, which may allow for both more father-son pairings or create more dangerous situations for the Peter Griffins of the world competing against youngsters with more energy, if not necessarily more ability. (Assumedly the more talented 20-somethings will be playing in some organized league —and it would not seem especially productive for a twenty-something seeking to catch a major-league scout's eye to do so against fantasy camp competition).

That the camps fill up year after year validates the demand. But from team's perspective, is it worth it? After all, the camps are labor intensive—Doug Dickey, who runs the Mets' fantasy camp, said the staffing includes him, five support staff (photographers, scorers and such), kitchen staff, clubhouse attendants, and four trainers, plus 25 coaches. Add to that the additional expenses involving the physical costs of running the facility where the camp is held, food for the week, and the hotel. Assumedly, part of a camper's bill goes directly to the hotel for their lodging, but the club must also foot the hotel bill for the staff flown in from the home city.

Doug Dickey and the 2019 New York Mets Fantasy Camp coaches (Photo courtesy of Marc Levine,Jennifer Voce-Nelson and Kayla Rice

For the privately-operated camps,that do make a profit, the net could be viewed as a decent sum. But for the teams that run their own fantasy operations, in the grand scheme of businesses that negotiate nine-figure player contracts and billion-dollar national television deals, why do they exert so much effort on a venture that at its best nets only a few hundred thousand dollars and serves, again at best, an incredible tiny percentage of the fan base?

The answer lies largely under the headings of public relations and goodwill.

"Obviously, it has a business model to make some money; however, if I were to say that is our only goal, I would be wrong," Dickey said. "Mets Fantasy Camp is an important program to have as it offers a unique experience that Mets fans can be a part of. It takes a lot of effort to run the camp, but the payoff supersedes the cost and labor needed to successfully execute the event. Not many people can say they've thrown on that Mets uniform and played on the same fields as their idols have. "

Jerry Lewis, who runs the Tigers' camp, said, "It has great PR benefits, as well as some financial," adding that through the camps, the team hopes to "renew the fan's love affair with the Tigers and Detroit growing up. Makes greater fans out of them."

"The Orioles do the camp as a 'PR tangent' of the club, a way to 'improve our Alumni Relations through our former pros and to 'make a bit of money' as well," the Baltimore club said in an email. "We would not be doing it if it were a financial drain, no matter how small the actual event."

Not to be overlooked is the additional benefit of maintaining close relations with former players, ties that can pay off in achieving willingness to participate in other public relations-type events that build further fan base goodwill.

"The alumni play a huge role in everything we do but especially Mets Fantasy Camp." Dickey said. "After all, without them, this program would not exist. Bringing the alumni down and giving them the opportunity to get to know the fans in this atmosphere is special. They are more relaxed, comfortable, and it makes it easier for the campers to interact with them."

One key to maintaining those relationships is input from the coaches in planning the general outlines of a camp. "I lean on their feedback to see if certain things we implement are working," Dickey said, "They are extra eyes and ears for me to gather information on how campers are reacting to things."

Making sure that the alumni have a good time is also very important, Lewis said, "since we have over 20 alumni each year and they love to attend as much as the campers. As they mix so well together with the common thread of being a former Tiger and its serves as a reunion for many. "

Jerry Lewis tries to make sure the Tigers Alumni have a good time. (Photo courtesy of Jerry Lewis)

But in the end, it is the campers' feedback that largely helps decide how future camps will be run. "It's really the campers we want to hear from," according to Lewis. "Over the course of 35 years, we have made many changes. We want to have the best camp for the best fans in the world. All suggestions are welcome."

Like any business, repeat customers are a yardstick, as well as positive word-of-mouth. "Feedback is my number one priority," Dickey said. "I take what the guys say very seriously and over the last six years that I have run the camp, I haven't had one formal complaint about the camp in its entirety. If the fans are happy, then we are. "

At least for Dickey, fantasy camp preparation is a year-round job. Once a year's event is over—the Mets have been running two one-week camps, back-to-back, starting in mid-January—Dickey begins working on the next one. "Locking in dates, hotel/catering contracts, the list goes on. Those are all my top priority when I first get back," he said. "Then it transitions into working out the pricing, packaging, and overall details of the camp. I implement something new every year, or try to, so that is the time I get that all organized. Then it's time to sell and sign people up over the summer. The busiest time for me usually starts right at the end of the season in October. I have a pre-camp trip to Florida to meet with the staff and make sure things are lining up like they should. "

One would think that baseball, as an industry that works together to achieve common goals and address common problems —so much so that there have been accusations of collusion by the Major League Players Association in dealing with free agents and calls over the years to relieve baseball of its antitrust exemption— would have, over the years, engaged in considerable notes exchanging among the teams and a sharing of what the general business world calls best practices.

Somewhat surprisingly, as baseball fantasy camp works its way through its fourth decade, as an organized effort, that was not generally the case. "Until recently, camp directors did not really communicate with each other," Dickey said. "For the past two years, fantasy camps have been a topic and opportunity to brainstorm with other teams at the Baseball Winter Meetings. This past year I physically attended the meetings and it was a very informative and positive experience.

"I've worked with the Reds and Royals in the past. All camps have their differences. Our camp has been very successful over the past five years largely because of how much we give back to our fans. We aren't the most expensive camp, yet we are not the cheapest. We have started trends seen at other camps and we've taken other's ideas and modified them for our program."

"I talk to several other camp directors as much as I can," Lewis said. "They have the same problems and just about the same itinerary as we do." And they also do not find they compete for coaches to help run the camp. In fact, Dickey notes that he and the Reds work together to secure former second baseman Doug Flynn, who played for both clubs and who plays a key role at the Mets' camps.

Dickey and Lewis, somewhat understandingly, were coy when asked how much the coaches get paid. "Enough for them to get them to attend and they all get paid the same," was Lewis's reply. Dickey demurred to provide an answer.

As time goes on, the definition of "enough" may change. A more appropriate question could be: is anything enough? The major-league players who currently participate in fantasy camps are, to some degree, from an era in which salaries were not great and offseason jobs were often necessary to make ends meet. The somewhat younger participants, who fared better in terms of compensation during their playing days, are not those who necessarily can live for the rest of their lives off of their playing day earnings, and for whom the combined lure of being paid a little of money and being able relive their youth is incentive enough to sign on.

But, the Orioles worry, "As the current professionals are so well compensated for their 'on-field' prowess, we believe it could possibly make doing the event more difficult because their compensation is so great."

The key to overcoming that obstacle is emphasizing the continuing ties between player and team. As the Orioles noted, "We'll work hard to keep the relationships going with our current pros so they may consider doing the Dream Week [what they call their fantasy camp] when their playing days are completed."

Which brings us back to Randy Hundley, who remained briefly in the game after his playing days were over, spending a year as a major-league coach and three years as a minor-league manager before returning to investment banking, baseball camps for children, and lunches with restaurant entrepreneurs who planted ideas into his head.

"It never gets old putting on a uniform," Hundley was quoted as saying in a 2010 article that is part of the Society of American Baseball Research's biography project. "I love doing camps and I love what everybody is getting out of it. We were a family who enjoyed playing together, and now to let other people enjoy that with us has really been a fantastic experience all these years."

Which also serves to validate Hundley's comments in that 1992 *Chicago Tribune* article in which he expressed some surprise to realize he was the father of baseball fantasy camp. "In one sense, it's such a simple idea, yet nobody else had done it."

# CHAPTER 6

## LIVING THE FANTASY - THE FINAL FRONTIER

For Mark, certainly, and most probably Josh, a sense of unreality fell over them as it was finally time to go to fantasy camp. The weight had been lost, the drills completed, the equipment updated and oiled. A journey 30 years in the making the final baseball journey was about to begin.

Mark and Josh's final team road trip began back at Long Island MacArthur Airport, where, 19 years before, on their first baseball travel escapade, they were nearly stranded on their way to Disney World, until Mark used the Cougars as potential poster children for broken promises and persuaded Delta Airlines to capitulate and discover the alternate flight plans that took them to Orlando by way of Newark.

No such issues arose this time, as the Southwest flight was on schedule. Mark and Josh arrived at the airport with plenty of time to spare; Mark was able to watch his equipment bag be loaded onto the plane and strike up conversations with three other fantasy-camp bound passengers, one of them Eric Tartaglione, who identified himself as a standup comedian. He did not disclose whether fantasy camp would become fodder for his next routine.

Josh and Mark sat together on the plane, but each allowed the other enough quiet time for Mark to be alone with his thoughts and muse about the import of the moment. Flashing through Mark's mind were the many miles spent together driving to from games and the fact that although they had spent many plane rides with Beth and Liana on family trips, only once before had they been on a plane as a pair.

That was in 2015, and baseball also was the precipitator. They were headed to Kansas City for the first two games of the Mets-Royals World Series. Josh was one of the Mets team employees feted to game tickets, airfare, and lodging as a team thank-you for their work, and he chose Mark to accompany him.

Reflecting on that trip while flying to West Palm Beach for fantasy camp, Mark once again reaffirmed in his mind the power of baseball in cementing his bond with Josh. After all, Josh could have asked many other people to join him but chose his father as his guest.

Josh and Mark on the way to Game 1 of the 2015 World Series.(Photo courtesy of Mark Rosenman)

Mark's mind then wandered to the last time the two were at Mets fantasy camp, when Mark asked Josh to tag along and help him with videos as part of Mark's reportage, and the encounter between Josh and Turk Wendell that planted the seeds for what was now Josh's 30th birthday present. Wendell had been a time-marker for their relationship: think back to the spring training when Josh and some of the other 11-year-old Commack Cougars sought Wendell's autograph and didn't get it until someone said, "Please?" Would they now end up playing on Wendell's team to close the circle?

Mark reviewed the run-up to the big week: the months of weekly workouts at an indoor facility to reawaken both their baseball skills to minimize the potential for embarrassment. Mark's excitement at being able to hit progressively more difficult pitching and watching Josh reawaken his fielding skills. The increased agility and stamina from Mark's weight loss.

Josh had expressed some apprehension to Mark, noting it had been a considerable amount of time since he had actually played in a game, facing live pitching, and making defensive plays and throws against the pressure of an advancing runner. Mark had assured Josh, just as he had over the years of coaching him, they he would perform just fine and that he believed Josh would certainly be in the running for fantasy camp Rookie of the Year.

But the prevailing emotion as they landed, selected their rental car and began the drive from West Palm Beach to Port St. Lucie, was more eager anticipation than maudlin nostalgia or abject fear of failure. Understood, but left unsaid in the moment, was that this was a last-in-a-lifetime experience with every precious second to be savored.

# DAY ONE: WORKOUTS AND WELCOMES

Crucial to fantasy week is perpetuating the illusion that the major league experience-not just the on-field, wearing-a-major-league-uniform, playing on the same fields as major leaguers experience-can be replicated for lawyers, accountants, computer programmers, firefighters, and the like with both the will and $5,000 wherewithal. Shower like a major leaguer! Trade insults just like major leaguers do! Be pampered by a trainer like major leaguers are! And best of all, actually do all of that with some of your favorite major leaguers! The only things missing are, to use the somewhat archaic phrase, Baseball Annies hanging around the hotel bar, although if the legality of what would be expected of them was not questionable, rest assured that, for a small additional fee, some enterprising major league front office staffer for one of the teams running a fantasy camp would have added them to the package, too.

For Mets fantasy camp, participants check into their Port St. Lucie hotel on Sunday of Fantasy Week. They get to visit the locker room-the dressing room at the club's minor league complex that is part of the Port St. Lucie spring training facility-try on the Mets home and road uniforms with their names and chosen numbers on the back and take part in unofficial workouts. No worries if the uniforms don't fit, tailors are standing by to make repairs. They also get to meet, in the most informal of settings, some of their coaches and former idols, who will not only be providing instruction but dressing with them.

Mark and Josh are assigned adjacent lockers next to former Mets catcher John Stearns, who is the Fantasy League commissioner, which means that he will spend the week walking from field to field, spinning stories and trying to make it appear that he has mastered the fantasy league rules.

Mark and Josh's lockers for the week. (Photo courtesy of Mark Rosenman)

With the exception of a few marquee names, most of the former major leaguers on hand had short-of-Hall-of-Fame careers and are remembered by only the most fanatical of Mets fans, i.e., the target market of current and future fantasy campers. But they do check the most important box in that they did reach the majors, and all have a list, however modest, of memorable major league achievements and baseball-behind-the-scenes yarns (Stearns is borderline marquee; his major-league career was solid and he was a star player, and a four time All-Star, on some not-very-good Mets teams from the mid-1970s to the mid-1980s ).

After the workouts, it's back to the hotel for the first of the feel-like-a-big-leaguer serendipities. It's an NFL playoff week, and the New Orleans Saints are playing the Philadelphia Eagles. Mets icon Ron Swoboda, who cemented his status as a permanent a fan favorite by making a spectacular catch in the 1969 World Series that help bring the Mets their improbable first championship, parks himself in front of a television in the hotel lobby to watch the game. Swoboda settled in New Orleans some years ago and became a popular sportscaster there; he is a rabid Saints fan.

Mark, and later Josh, join Swoboda in the lobby. Other campers trickle in to plop down on the couches around the television, and then follow a stream of the people they paid their money to see. First is Todd Pratt, a catcher whose memorable Met moment was a series-ending walk-off home run against the Arizona Diamondbacks in a 1999 playoff game. Pratt commandeers a chair and engages Swoboda in conversation on a variety of baseball topics, which lead to reminiscences about favorite baseball moments, not all of them on-field accomplishments. The talk turns to practical jokes and low moments in their teammates' off-field lives. Within a short period of time, some of the other coaches join the fray: Lenny Harris, a utility player who made his mark as a pinch-hitter extraordinaire, setting the record for hits in that category; Rodney McCray, an outfielder who literally ran through a minor-league fence chasing a fly ball (the video would be replayed for years after that in as the intro to a New York sportscaster's monthly segment of sports oddities); Buzz Capra, a pitcher on the 1973 pennant winner (most memorably for him marked by a playoff scuffle with Reds pitcher Pedro Borbon that resulted in the Cincinnati hurler ripping Capra's hat with his teeth) who enjoyed the best two years of his brief major-league career as an Atlanta Brave; Duffy Dyer, a backup catcher and Swoboda's teammate on the 1969 championship squad, and Ed Hearn, a backup catcher on the 1986 championship team who overcame serious health issues after his playing career ended and who has become a successful motivational speaker.

Harris brings to the conversation a lifetime of baseball knowledge and stories. McCray brings energy; he is a college football aficionado with incredible knowledge of that sport and the ability to generate a debate over hated football coaches (starting with Nick Saban and, in a room of New Yorkers, naturally the New England Patriots' Bill Belichick becomes a central figure) and carry it through.

The NFL game on the screen becomes secondary. With the exception of Swoboda, the assembled are not focusing on what was becoming an exciting and close football game. They are observing, and taking part, in the back-and-forth and lest they miss the significance of the moment, Pratt-who segued into becoming the unofficial moderator of the conversation-announces to the campers: "This is what really goes on in the major leagues!"

The week officially begins that evening with a welcoming dinner at a Port St. Lucie country club, and a program emceed by former Mets second baseman Doug Flynn. He intersperses his remarks with frequent references to injuries and the need to avoid them, putting into context the appropriateness of the week's corporate sponsor: The Hospital for Special Surgery. Manager Mickey Callaway makes a brief appearance-as had his predecessor, Terry Collins, in previous years-to whip the room of Mets fanatics into a frenzy about the upcoming season.

Callaway sets the tone for the week when he tells the audience there are two major goals for them: first, don't get hurt; and, second, don't bat out of order. That prompts the expected laugh; it is a self-deprecating reference to the low point of Callaway's rookie managerial year, when he posted a lineup in the dugout different from the one he handed the umpires, resulting in a successful challenge that erased a scoring opportunity. The gaffe came in the midst of a multi-game swoon from which the team spent the rest of the year trying to recover from.

"Don't bat out of order" (Photo courtesy of Marc Levine,Jennifer Voce-Nelson and Kayla Rice )

Flynn notes that among the week's events will be a charity raffle. The beneficiary will be the daughter of the late Mets pitcher Anthony Young, who endeared himself to the fanbase by his good humor and stoicism in losing 29 games in a row. Young, a frequent and popular coach at Mets fantasy camp, passed away in June 2017; the daughter is to pursue premed studies and tuition assistance will be welcomed.

Flynn reels off the roster of coaches for the week. The clear headliner is Dwight Gooden, both in terms of his accomplishments and his places in Mets fans' hearts. The players essentially span the whole gamut of Mets history, from Felix Millan, who played second base on the 1973 "You Gotta Believe" pennant winners, to more recent alumni such as Heath Bell, Steve  Trachsel, and Nelson Figueroa. Swoboda and Dyer, the representatives from the 1969 championship team, are introduced last, allowing a plug for the upcoming weekend marking the 50th anniversary of that improbable run. Never let it be said that a marketing opportunity was missed.

After dinner, Flynn goes around the room and asks the newbies in the crowd to introduce themselves. What is most striking is how few of the 111 players at the camp are first-timers, only 12. Most of the first-timers, it seems, come from New Jersey. But among the others who stand up are players from Illinois and Idaho. Some, like Las Vegas-area paramedic and ambulance company owner Brian Rogers, are transplanted New Yorkers (he is a former New York City firefighter). For others, their Mets fandom origin is less clear. One camper, from Long Beach on Long Island, mentions that he is there with his father and his brother.

All speak of their excitement as playing with and for their baseball idols and speak of expected on-field accomplishments in the upcoming week. When Flynn points the microphone in Josh's direction, he notes a different objective. His goal, he tells the audience to much laughter, is that his mother sent him down to keep his father from hurting himself as badly as he had in fantasy camps past.

Josh at the Welcome Dinner explaining his goal for the week. (Photo courtesy of Marc Levine,Jennifer Voce-Nelson and Kayla Rice )

\*\*\*\*\*\*

So who, exactly, goes to fantasy camp, and why do they keep on coming back?

Geographically, the largest representation among the 111 campers is from New Jersey, 29, followed by 22 from New York City, 18 from Long Island, 13 from Florida, six from Westchester and points north, and four from Connecticut. The distribution would seem somewhat surprising-the common wisdom is that New Jerseyites are more Yankees fans than Mets' (as, too, it is believed, are Connecticut residents, making that group's meager representation understandable). The explanation, as was learned in conversations with the players, lies in New York City childhoods before becoming Garden State transplants, or fathers who were city dwellers or Long Islanders who inculcated their Mets fandom in their progeny.

The depth of that fandom also become clear in looking at the more exotic representations: Virginia (two), Pennsylvania (two), Massachusetts (two), Nevada (two), among other states, but also Saskatoon. Saskatchewan, England, and Venezuela.

Josh is one of two minimum-age campers (30); the age spread goes into the high 60s. Nor are he and Mark the only father-son pairing, or the only relatives. Brothers and some cousins are among the counted.

One of the more far-flung travelers, and a repeat camper, was Shane McDonald. Shane grew up in Saskatchewan, Canada, which would seem to be an unusual place to find a baseball fan, let alone one whose team of choice is the New York Mets. But as he tells the story, when he got his first pack of baseball cards, he decided he would root for whatever team the first player in the pack represented, It was a Topps 1970 card of  Mets hurler Jerry Koosman.

Fast forward a few decades. Shane went on to a career in computer programming, then on to teaching computer programming. As he was about to turn 50, his wife was looking for a special half-century birthday present. She sent him to Mets fantasy camp, and he was hooked. He returned two years later and again two years after that.

Shane McDonald and his expensive Jerry Koosman baseball card.(Photo courtesy of Shane McDonald)

The Charroux family-father Carl and son Cameron-came from both sides of the continent. Carl Charroux grew up in Massachusetts but now lives in Los Angeles; son Cameron still lives in the Bay State. Cameron is a database administrator; Carl, now in his mid-50s, describes his occupation simply as "technology," although he allows that he has dabbled in acting and did "some work in television." (His IMDB mini-bio describes him as an actor and director known for the soap operas *One Life to Live* and *All My Children* in the late 1960s and as the writer/producer/

director of the short 2011 action comedy "*Custody*," which had a shelf life even shorter than its running time of 11 minutes.

Carl attributes his Mets fandom to cable television and the advent of super stations, in particular New York station WOR, the channel that carried Mets telecasts for decades. "I got interested in the Mets in the 70's because they were on WOR. Cable had just come out, so I got to see this team I had never seen before," he recalled. "I started following them." And, he noted, "I gave my son the disease. I just passed it on."

Thirty-one-year-old Cameron notes that baseball has played an important role in their relationship. While he did not play high school baseball-"I broke my arm and my baseball career came tumbling down"-he frequently watched his father play softball. And baseball continues to be the framework for daily conversations, especially now that their relationship is bi-coastal. "It's very important," Carl noted. To which Cameron added, "We Face Time now on the phone. I'm literally taking swings in the backyard (preparing for fantasy camp) and he's critiquing me - work on this, no, no. He's got this look on his face of total disgust."

Fantasy camp was Carl's instigation. "I always wanted to go for years, and finally was able to do it financially, so forth and so on." That was four years ago, and in true Hollywood style, the former actor brought his entourage with him-his wife, his daughter and his father, also named Carl, who now lives in Florida but who still has his distinct Boston accent. "They've been down here all four years. Even just watching, they fell in love with the whole thing. "

And when Cameron hit the minimum age to play last year, Carl was excited about being able to play with his son, although he does note differences between him and his offspring. "The big difference is I'm so damned competitive and he's not. I will try to win everything. He's more easygoing about it. But the bonding of just having a conversation and both of us having these conversations with the pros ... playing together is great, but so is the total experience."

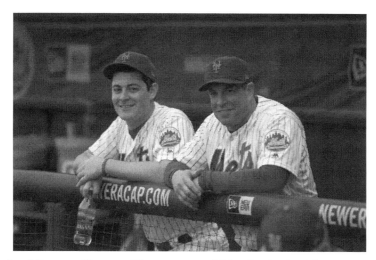

Carl and Cameron Charroux (Photo courtesy of Marc Levine ,Jennifer Voce-Nelson and Kayla Rice )

It may be delayed reaction, but listening to Cameron, a little bit of his father rubbed off. "The first time was having the experience, going with him, having fun" he said. "This year, I want to win."

Which brings us to the Reale brothers, Andrew and David. Andrew lives in Wayne, New Jersey, and he and his brother work in the family business, a company that manufactures ornamental and structural stainless steel tubing founded by their father. Andrew, the older brother, is the CEO. David, the younger, is the better athlete, although not by much, a fact that will come to light a few days later at the farewell breakfast when it was revealed that David was the first overall pick in the draft.

They are at their 18th or 19th fantasy camp. The first one, as Andrew tells it, was his idea. "I saw the commercials," he said. "I called and said my brother and I want to go. They said, 'how old are you?' and I said, '30.' They said, 'How old is your brother?' I said 27." It only took about four repetitions of the question for

Andrew to pick up on the hint and say that David, like he, was over the minimum age.

Just like Carl Charroux, the Reales went to their first fantasy camp with their competitive juices flowing. "The first fantasy camp, I wanted to beat everybody," Andrew said. "These guys were so good, I hated it. I noticed definitely, there were rivalries going on." Eighteen camps later? "It's like a lovefest."

Unlike other family pairings, the Reales do not play on the same team. That is because, as Andrew noted, they spend enough time together at work and have played softball together. Playing against one another is a well-appreciated change.

The Reales continue in their Grandfather's footsteps. (Photo courtesy of The Reale Family )

Their Mets fandom stemmed from their grandfather, who played baseball and who regaled his grandsons with stories about playing baseball while in the service during World War II (including against Yankees great and Hall of Famer Phil Rizzuto. And one of the original lures of fantasy camp was the ability for their grandfather, who had retired to Florida, to see them play.

But what also drew them in, as the organizers of all the fantasy camps hope, was the opportunity to hobnob with their former idols. "My brother and I couldn't believe the coaches, how nice they were," he said, "You could go off with them, you could have a drink with them, go to dinner with them. That definitely was a big part of why we decided to come back."

And if they had any doubts about the decision, those doubts vanished when they arrived at the airport for Year Two and went to retrieve their luggage. Waiting near the baggage carousels was 1969 World Series hero Ron Swoboda. "He said, Hi, Andy, how are you doing?"

They were hooked.

\*\*\*\*\*

## DAY 2: EVALUATIONS AND THE GAMES BEGIN

Day two begins with evaluations: batting practice pitched by some of the former major-league hurlers; infield drills monitored, and coached, by former basemen and shortstops; pitching in the cages and running exercises. Throughout it all, the managers for each of the 10 teams float among the stations and the practice fields, taking notes on clipboards and comparing them with their co-managers and opposing skippers. Some, such as Swoboda, are intensely serious. Other, such as former Mets starter Steve Trachsel (nicknamed the Human Rain Delay for the deliberate manner in which the plied his craft on the mound) and catcher Barry Lyons are looser and more loquacious as they lean on backstops and survey the talent or lack thereof on the field.

With so many returning campers, and so many mangers familiar with their abilities, the managers focus their attention on the first-timers, looking to discover the player or player who might go unnoticed by their competing managers.

Doug Flynn works out the infielders during evaluations . (Photo courtesy of Marc Levine,Jennifer Voce-Nelson and Kayla Rice )

As the campers eat lunch in a large tent, helping themselves to assorted cold cuts, salads, and a few hot dishes, the managers retire to a conference area for the player draft.

While each managerial team will have its own strategy, universal is the fantasy league extension of the major league maxim: You can't have enough pitching. The pitchers will go first, especially those who can-more often in this order than not-throw strikes and bring some degree of velocity. Josh would have been one of those, except for a fantasy camp rule that sets a minimum age of 35 to pitch. This is understandably designed to protect some of the older campers whose advancing age has slowed their reaction times.

The managers must also consider draft "entries"-father-son pairings who are guaranteed placement on the same team and others who have requested they play together because they are longtime friends back home (and, perhaps, because one has convinced the other to join him). Ideally, the pairs should be close in ability to warrant a pick based on the better of the two, because in choosing an entry, the manager forfeits his choice in the next round.

Mark and Josh believe they will be selected somewhere in the middle of the draft-the allure of Josh's youth and ability tempered by Mark's age and average overall skills.

After about 90 minutes, figurative white smoke rises from the conference area and the coaches emerge to announce their teams-and their team nicknames. Some of the nicknames played on the managers' names, occasionally incorporating other subtle references (Team L&B, managed by Barry Lyons and Kevin Baez, also evokes a famous Brooklyn pizzeria). Heath Bell nicknames his team Bell's Ringers. Turk Wendell and Ed Hearn nickname their team The Good Doctors, which at first blush seemed like an homage to named sponsor Hospital for Special Surgery but which, it turned out, was based on an erroneous belief that their roster would be populated by vacationing medical personnel.

As each set of coaches disclose their rosters, the players stand when their names are called and survey the room to locate teammates. The returnees-the bulk of the campers-can immediately begin sizing up their squads and their relative chances of success.

Mark and Josh become Citi Slickers (a play on Citi Field, where the Mets play, and the Billy Crystal film whose plot is essentially about cattle ranching fantasy camp). Their coaches are two former Mets pitchers who typify the profile of the major league staff with modest but exciting-to-Mets-fans resumes: Pete Schourek and Eric Hillman. They were teammates on early 1990s Mets squads remembered largely for turmoil and the failure of some high-priced free agents and they achieved greater success after leaving the Mets: Schourek pitching for the Cincinnati Reds and Hillman in Japan, where his six-foot-ten-inch-frame made him especially noticeable.

Eric Hillman announcing the Citi Slickers roster. (Photo courtesy of Marc Levine,Jennifer Voce-Nelson and Kayla Rice )

Mark is excited to be playing for them, especially Hillman, whose interview appearance in the early days of Mark's radio show remains one of the most memorable for its humor and outrageousness. Hillman also coached Mark in his first fantasy camp. Eric is energetic, upbeat, witty and, it will be noted after a conversation a few days later, perceptive. Schourek is quieter and earnest.

As for his teammates, Mark looks around the tent at those who stood when Hillman called their name and pronounces: "We have a stacked team." The Citi Slickers, it turns out, have some heavy hitters, both literally and figuratively. One, Phil Forman, has participated in many consecutive fantasy camp final games, plays a stellar shortstop has a reputation as a great teammate. At least three -- including fantasy camp veterans Dave Helfrich, Seth Davis and Bobby Whelan–can pitch, Mark notes. All of the players appear capable of carrying their weight. By the end of the week, as the pulled muscles mounted, a more appropriate nickname for the team would be Last Man Standing.

The Citi Slickers would have only moments to make acquaintances and ruminate about their individual assessments of their squad before the first game begins. A first-time fantasy camp observer notes one of the most obvious differences between fantasy and major league baseball: a rolling screen posted only a few feet behind the catcher to minimize the distance needed to chase passed balls and most wild pitches.

Hillman calls the team together for some brief inspirational remarks before they take the field. "Stay relaxed," he says. "And stay healthy."

The game starts with both Rosenmans in the outfield-Mark in right and Josh in center. It is the first time in all his years of playing baseball that Josh has been asked to play center-he was mostly a third baseman and a pitcher-and he has never been considered fleet enough of foot to cover the ground required to the position. But in a nod to the maxim that everything is relative, Hillman has made the understandable judgment that because of his youth, Josh will nevertheless be able to cover more ground that his mid-life teammates.

The Citi Slickers get off to an auspicious start, barraging The Good Doctors with 23 hits in a 12-3 romp. Forman, as billed, proves to be a capable shortstop; Davis, who is second to Josh in youth, fulfills the major goal of a fantasy league pitcher: get the ball over the plate; and Helfrich channels Keith Hernandez with some baserunner-saving scoops at first. Ordinarily, the correct term would be "error-saving," but in fantasy league scoring, there are no errors, just failures to get a batter out.

Under this relaxed scoring system, Josh goes 2-for-3; under any scoring, he was robbed of a third hit –although he did get the team's first run batted in-by some baserunning misadventures.

Mark goes 1-for-2; another at-bat sets the table for him becoming the Mets fantasy camp version of Ron Hunt (or Craig Biggio or Don Baylor) with the first of what will be several hit-by-pitches.

The game is also notable for Davis picking off a Good Doctor, prompting a call for Commissioner Stearns to issue a rules interpretation about whether in a game where stealing is not allowed, pickoffs are. After consulting the rulebook (which is in every campers' welcome packet), the judgment is that a runner can be picked off, a point Stearns returns repeatedly to emphasize with any coaches who happen to be listening. Assumedly, he has also made this point on the other four fields.

Mark and Josh retire to their hotel room with visions of championship trophies dancing in their heads as they prepare for a dinner with their team.

******

The fantasy camp experience is not one-way. While the campers get to live the what they believe is the major league experience, those who really know-the coaches-get from the week as much as they give.

On one level, putting on uniforms and spikes transports them back to what they nostalgically remember as happier times, an annual reunion that allows stories to be retold and laughs to be shared anew. On a different level, being remembered and feted by fans reaffirms that for a period time, longer for some and brief for others but real nevertheless, their careers were meaningful, at least to the most fanatical of fans, and that their accomplishments have not been forgotten.

But, and this may seem somewhat surprising, the coaches come away from fantasy camp with the same rewards as the campers, noting friendships made and renewed annually. If there is a fantasy camp club, its membership is not limited to the paying customers. Their roles are different, but they are equals.

Think of it like the relationship between a student and his or her favorite high school teacher. As the student matures, goes off to college, and sets off on life as an adult, former student and teacher remain in touch the bond morphs into one of more of equals than mentor-tutee.

So when you ask Pete Schourek, now in his eighth or ninth Mets fantasy camp, why he keeps coming back, the former major-league hurler says, "For the camaraderie. The overwhelming pride I feel in these guys, why they just give every single bit of energy throughout the whole week, no matter how broken down they get. They just love playing the game."

Or former Mets reliever Turk Wendell-best remembered for his quirks that included brushing his teeth between innings and jumping over the baselines rather than stepping on them-on why he is in his seventh camp: "I have a lot of fun meeting fans on a more intimate basis ... and you meet some really good people, some interesting people, who are friends for the rest of your life."

Wendell adds, "I think a lot of the players, speaking just for myself, get as much out of it as the campers get out of it."

If there is a philosopher among the 23 coaches, or anyone who could be called deep thinker, it is Hillman, who when asked about the biggest takeaway for the campers, responds, "The fact that this game is the great equalizer. This game brings people together; it brings white collar, it brings blue collar, it brings CEOs and average Joes together on one team. They bond, they have fun, they go out and they fight every game.'

"The game brings people together" ((Photo courtesy of Marc Levine,Jennifer Voce-Nelson and Kayla Rice )

"We've had ballplayers come down here and they've got more money than God and they're on a team with a guy who's making 35, 40 grand a year who's lucky enough to get this gift of a birthday present, and they save $50 a paycheck for the next five years in order to come back down here again. This game-it doesn't care who you are, it doesn't care how much money you have, it doesn't care what neighborhood you live in. But we have people who for the most part aren't going to be running in the same social circles, they aren't going to be eating in the same restaurants, and they come down here and they bond, over their love of baseball, and over their love of the New York Mets. And all of a sudden, the fast friendships and the fast bonds that are created by going out and competing together -that is what is truly amazing."

To punctuate his point that this is one aspect in which fantasy camp parallels reality, Hillman draws from his own life and his relationship with the late Anthony Young, who became a fan favorite by setting the record for futility in losing-with a lot of bad luck but a considerable amount of grace-29 losses in a row. As a former fantasy camp coach, Young's ghost casts an on-and-off shadow throughout this camp.

"Anthony Young was from Houston. He was an absolute brother to me," Hillman says. "I had a chance to know him for 30 years. I was very fortunate; some of those guys only got to know him for one, two, or three years, maybe. I feel fortunate to have had him for 30 years. But here's a guy who grew up in the bad part of Houston, and I grew up in Chicago, and the next thing you know, we're the same thing, people from two different demographics who were thrown together, played ball together, went out and fought teams together and we developed these great absolute friendships."

Schourek, Wendell, and Hillman are especially aware of the family pairings who make their way to the camp. "It's really cool to see the fathers have so much invested in everything the son does," Schourek says." That's really cool because I have kids and I can feel the same way. It makes me feel how proud my dad was, so I got to live in those shoes."

Joe Schourek was a respected teacher and successful baseball coach as a Washington, DC.-area high school who coached his son in Little League and teenage travel ball. As an aside, Pete Schourek notes, "I've never had a coach that was harder than my dad. He knew how to push me properly. He knew I didn't need to be coddled." Joe was there for Pete's first major-league game, and Pete and Joe Schourek still talk once a week, although the conversation turns more to the grandchildren than to baseball.

In terms of father-son relationships among the fantasy campers, Hillman particularly appreciates what Mark and Josh went through to get to camp, especially their weight loss regimens. While he drafted the team because of Josh, he noted, "I also saw that Mark had lost about 35 pounds." And, somewhat wistfully, he notes the difference between the Mark-Josh relationship and the ones he has had with his father (who did throw batting practice to him when he was young but was sporadic about making it to his games) or with his own sons, now 19 and 21 years old, neither of whom played baseball or is a fan. "They're skiers," he said. "It really doesn't bother me at all. They asked me, Dad, is it really okay that we don't really play baseball or basketball or hockey like you did as a kid? And I said, 'Not at all, because you guys can ski a lot longer than you can play any of those activities."

Of all the facets to the fantasy camp experience, Schourek, Wendell and Hillman were unanimous that the one that most replicates the big leagues in the grind of playing so many games in so few days.

"It's showing up to the field every single day, whether it's raining or not," Schourek says. "Just the fact that you are here every day, getting treatment in the training room. The food is exactly what we did in spring training, they're living the exact same thing that we did."

"I try to get the players to understand that basically they play Monday, Tuesday, Wednesday, Thursday-four days," Wendell says. "Try doing this for 192 games in a row. For seven and a half to eight months, you're doing this every day. You've got aches and pains and you're whining about stuff for three or four days? Really?. So that's just a different perspective, and that's just playing the games. It's not counting the travel. That's not counting being away from your family for that long, missing your kids grow up."

For Hillman, at least returning to fantasy camp gives him perspective-on his career and on life.

"I'll be 53 in April and I came here [to Mets spring training] for the very first time as a 21-year-old, with my entire career ahead of me, and the reason I made it to the major leagues was I knew that when I walked in that gate as a 21-year-old I knew that I was going to be pitching in New York.

"I played with a lot of guys who were overwhelmed to be here as a minor league ballplayer. They saw they were professional baseball players and they thought that was the greatest thing since sliced bread, and then I played with guys who were overwhelmed by going to Double A, overwhelmed by going to Triple A, they didn't think they were going to get that far. Myself and Pete [Schourek] were always extremely confident in ourselves, we were never arrogant. We always spoke with, this is who we are, we are just going to go out and play. We're going to compete. That's what I expected of myself from the time I was in second grade. I expected to play at this level. I wasn't overwhelmed or surprised by getting there because I had visualized, I had seen in my head over and over and over again that this is where I wanted to be and this is where I thought I deserved to be."

So returning to Port St. Lucie, she said, gives him "appreciation for the road that I did hoe."

But the biggest perspective? "I get it when you fly into a city, and you have a window seat. You're sitting there, whether it's Atlanta, Chicago, Kansas City, Detroit, no matter where you fly into, baseball fields are real easy to see from the sky. You fly into these other large metropolises and you see those baseball fields, and you know there are kids on those baseball fields, the same way I was on my Little League fields ... and the vast majority of all those kids on all of those different fields....you know every one of those kids wants to play in the major leagues, whatever team they are a fan of to be in that region.

"So for me to be humbled enough to know that I had the opportunity to play at that level is amazing, and it amazes me."

## DAYS THREE THROUGH FIVE: THE GAMES
## CONTINUE AND REALITY SETS IN

It didn't take long for Mark and Josh to come back to earth. Just as they blew out The Good Doctors in their first game, the Citi Slickers were blown out in the second, 14—3. They rallied to take the afternoon contest, 2—1, with Josh doing his best Tommie Agee impression in center field, chasing a ball to the fence (fastest I have seen him run, Mark would say afterward) and beginning a relay that would nail a runner at home plate and keep the score 1—0. Josh would go 2-for-3, plus a walk and a hit-by- pitch. Mark went 1-for-4; yes, he, too, took one for the team.

That evening, the entire camp participated in a "bull session"- a larger, more formal version of the Sunday gathering around the hotel lobby television-and a raffle in which the prizes were current and past Mets' memorabilia. The previous year, the raffle raised $40,000, with the money going to cancer research in the name of Anthony Young, who fell victim to the disease a few months later. As noted at the welcome dinner, some of the 2018 proceeds would go to help fund college tuition for Young's daughter.

As Wednesday's games started, the Citi Slickers were still mathematically in contention for a playoff spot, and that dream continued through the morning's tilt, which provided the highlight of Josh hitting a home run, a prodigious blast that nearly cleared the fence and was far enough from the fielders for Josh to round the bases comfortably (if not easily). The pitcher: comedian Jim Breuer, a longtime fantasy camper who would leave before the end of the week to perform. While happy over his accomplishment, Josh took the dinger in stride. Proud pop Mark, however, took to Facebook and Twitter to gush about how this was the proudest moment of his entire baseball career with Josh.

Josh holding signed line-up card commemorating his home run . (Photo courtesy of
Marc Levine,Jennifer Voce-Nelson and Kayla Rice )

Again, everybody would come back to earth in the afternoon game, and injuries were beginning to take their toll. The Citi Slickers were becoming regulars in the trainer's room, and many needed the benefit of courtesy runners because they could not physically run the 90 feet from home to first, let alone around the bases if necessary.

In that, they were no different than other teams in this, or previous fantasy camps. Davis would note a few nights later that, as one of the younger and more physically fit participants, he had often been called on to run for teammates beset by groin pulls and muscle soreness.

After losing to (Rodney) McCray's Hotshots, the Citi Slickers were eliminated from the semifinals and would play out the string in Thursday's games for fun, pride, and individual accomplishments.

The stat sheet after the five games would show Josh with a hefty .786 batting average and seven RBIs, putting him in the running for both the batting title and Rookie of the Year. Mark was hitting a more modest .250, but he was equal to Josh in one category: both had been hit twice by pitches.

The evening's entertainment was the "kangaroo court," another simulation of the major league experience which, like its real-life counterpart, serves to bond teammates through humor. Players-in this case campers-are accused of petty infractions and fined for their transgressions after a "hearing" in which another player or players are designated as judges.

In the case of fantasy camp kangaroo court, the coaches serve as the tribunal, although the campers are encouraged to report actionable sins. An example: Bill Waschenko broke the rule prohibiting alcohol in the locker room ($5) and the more egregious offense of refusing to share with the coaches ($5 for each of the 21 coaches). Retired New York City policeman Carl Randazzo paid a hefty price for a social media gaffe: while professing to be a diehard and supremely loyal Mets fan, his Facebook page included a photograph-projected on a screen for all to see-of him wearing a New York Yankees jersey. The fine-$5 for each pinstripe on the offending Bronx Bomber shirt-was levied without any opportunity for explanation, not that any would have mitigated the offense.

At five dollars a stripe, Carl's fine was pretty hefty. (Photo courtesy of Carl Randazzo )

One of the campers, in an effort to turn the tables on the tribunal, did exact a small manner of revenge. The comedian Jim Breuer, who served up Josh's home run ball, parodied an on field rant by Duffy Dyer, the 1969 Met backup catcher known to repeat Mets fantasy campers for his loud and long outbursts. The impression produced laughter even from Dyer, so close was it to the real thing.

Jim Breuer turns the table on the court. (Photo courtesy of Marc Levine,Jennifer Voce-Nelson and Kayla Rice )

For the Citi Slickers, the Thursday games were a limp to the finish line. Even the courtesy runners are nursing aches and pains, so much so that at one point, Schourek takes to the basepaths on behalf of one of his hurting charges. He will be thrown out on a play at home plate in which, demonstrating that he had learned from watching the previous five games, he does not risk injury by attempting to slide. Mark's groin is barking; he has spent much time in the trainer's room and will sit out parts of the final game. Josh, too, complains of tightness in his left leg and he, too, will sit out an inning in the field.

The Citi Slickers are not alone. At all of the fields, the trainers are as much of a presence as the umpires, with the campers valiantly soldiering on. At one field, a trainer can be seen talking to a catcher: "There is no real taping technique. You just jammed it. After the game, come in." At another point, someone observes, "This is a war of attrition."

## DAY SIX (PART ONE): THE FINAL FANTASY

For some of the campers-especially those who did not get to play in the championship game-the final fantasy experience will come when they get to play three innings on First Data Field, the stadium where the Mets play their spring training games, against some of their coaches (the championship competitors got to play under the lights the night before at First Data, with a public address announcer and other professional simulations).

This exercise serves dual purposes, perpetuating the illusion that the campers might, in their day, have been good enough to warrant a near-major-league experience while at the same time reminding them of the significant talent gap between them and their major league mentors.

For Mark and Josh, the intimidation begins even before the Citi Slickers' assigned three-inning slot, as they arrive at First Data field and see former major-league reliever Heath Bell showing little mercy to the Slickers' predecessors. Bell's pitches are hitting the mid-80 mph mark on the radar gun, ominously displayed on the First Data scoreboard. Conversely, the major leaguers demonstrate how little they fear campers' pitching by shunning helmets when it is their turn at the plate.

Heath Bell showing no mercy on the hill. (Photo courtesy of Marc Levine,Jennifer Voce-Nelson and Kayla Rice )

Hillman and Schourek offer Josh the opportunity to pitch; while fantasy camp rules do not allow anyone under 30 to take the mound against campers, the prohibition does not apply to the major leaguers. Josh eagerly accepts the invitation Hillman slots him into the rotation just after the previous pitcher, facing Turk Wendell, hurls one of the specially taped apples that is part of the traditional merriment. One big splat, and here comes Josh, who breaks off a few decent curveballs to Doug Dickey, the fantasy camp director (not a former major leaguer, but a career Mets employee) before laying one in to light-hitting infielder Kevin Baez, who failed to clear the fences in his brief Mets career but nearly did it against Josh.

This is the same Kevin Baez who ran winter clinics for the 10-year-old Commack Cougars, but nostalgia was not why Josh seemed to be taking it easy on his former tutor. Josh would note afterward that he was holding back on his pitches because the opposition was not wearing helmets and he feared his control might have been an issue had been throwing harder. Mark kvelled nevertheless.

Josh Rosenman back on the mound. (Photo courtesy of Marc Levine,Jennifer Voce-Nelson and Kayla Rice ))

When their turn to bat came, Nelson Figueroa, a journeyman major leaguer whose seven-team major league odyssey included some memorable Mets moments, was on the mound. Josh popped out. Asked to recall his at bat afterward, Mark ticked off what to him was an epic struggle: taking an 80-mph fastball, outside, then second fastball, low. A third fastball, 81 mph, nicking the outside of the plate. Finally, a curveball would produce the highlight of the at-bat: a not-so-loud foul. And finally, a fastball that froze Mark as it caught the plate. Good morning, good afternoon, have some tea, good night.

The final score: Real Guys 6, Citi Slickers 0.

Good Morning, Good Afternoon, have some tea, Good Night. ((Photo courtesy
of Marc Levine,Jennifer Voce-Nelson and Kayla Rice )

## DAY SIX (PART TWO): ACCOLADES AND FAREWELLS

The week comes to an official end with an awards banquet, and
unlike the welcoming repast five days earlier, which had open
seating, players sit with their teams. This is crucial to the program
and to their recognition by their coaches and their peers. As they
wait for the festivities to begin, the campers trade email addresses
and pledges to remain in contact. They will also present envelopes
to their coaches, the result of collections taken to at least provide
their former heroes and now new friends with beer money for their
long trips home. They will similarly thank their bus driver-who
will get the biggest ovation of the evening-and, perhaps most
importantly to them, the training staff. The trainers would seem to
have produced the most worthy accomplishment: neither a crutch
nor a cast is in sight.

Balls are passed around for autographs-not those of the former
major leaguers (there is no need, since each of the campers will

receive a miniature home plate painstakingly inked by all of the coaches),-but by their teammates, part of their individual 2019 fantasy camp chronicle. Already, the anecdotes that will find their way into fantasy camp lore are being recounted among the campers, in a test of their universality and potential staying power.

One by one, the teams are called. The coaches take to the stage to announce each team's most valuable player.

Interspersed with the team MVP announcements are camp-wide awards in a number of different categories, most of them statistically based. However, keeping with the tone of the week, the first award is one named after former longtime Mets trainer Tom McKenna.

As Doug Flynn, emceeing the closing ceremonies as he had the welcoming dinner, notes, "This award will go to a player who has spent a great deal of time in the training room. They have been able to persevere, get fixed up and then go out and continue to play and enjoy the week."

The competition is stiff and the finalists worthy, the presenter, Dr. David Phearson (from the Hospital for Special Surgery) notes in detailing their near-winning maladies: Michael Tuller suffered a laceration when hit by a thrown bat while backing up first base; the player who showed up with knee problems and battled through the week; Gary Peterson broke his nose in the championship game and went back to play. The winner: Citi Slicker Bob Ghani, who "got tangled up in the grass and took a fall, bruised his knee pretty bad. It was swollen, black and blue and every other color of the rainbow." It was not his only injury of the week: he also played with a hurt thigh muscle. All of which explains why he was one of the Citi Slickers who needed a courtesy runner, starting about halfway through the games, and why he served as designated hitter more than he played the field.

Mark and Josh join their teammates in cheering as he limps to the stage to accept his award.

Over the next 90 minutes, each of the teams will be recognized, with each of the players being asked to stand as they are named. The coaches will then announce which of their charges they have chosen as the team's most valuable player, after remarks summarizing the highs and lows of their week and the togetherness the experience breeds.

Typical was the comment by former Mets catcher Todd Pratt, coaching for his sixth year, who noted, "This is what it's all about. It's meeting new people and getting to know personalities and becoming family. The first year, it's about baseball and let's do good. The second year, it's starting to know people, or at least introducing yourself to people. And the third year is when I really start feeling part of the family. I felt like that from day one."

Interspersed between the team introductions and MVP announcements are the camp-wide awards, most of them statistical: hits, pitching, fielding. Josh is a runner-up for Rookie of the Year, but he wins the batting title, his .786 average barely beats out teammate Dave Helfrich, a fantasy camp regular. Josh's acceptance speech is short: "I want to thank my dad and mom for an awesome 30th birthday gift" is his entire oration. Mark trails Josh as he walks up to accept the award, stopping just short of the stage so he is close enough to record Lenny Harris presenting the award on his iPhone. As happy as Josh is, Mark seems even happier; as he posts the video and still photo on Facebook, he will note that this was "the end to a perfect week."

Lenny Harris presenting Josh with the Cleon Jones Award. (Photo courtesy of Marc Levine,Jennifer Voce-Nelson and Kayla Rice )

While for Mark, Josh's award may have been the end of the week, it wasn't the end of the awards ceremony. And two other recognitions were notable. The first was the "Good Guy" award, named in memory of Anthony Young, a recounting of whose accomplishments both as a major-league teammate and as a fantasy week coach continued as a recurring theme.

And it was left to Hillman, in presenting the award, to perform the final evocation of Young's accomplishments and the encapsulation of his life.

"I feel very fortunate to have known AY," Hillman said, using the former pitcher's in-house nickname. "I got to know AY for over 30 years. We were both drafted in 1987. Pete Schourek was in that draft as well. I used to say AY and I were brothers ... our mom fooled around a lot [laughter from the audience, as expected]...When you think of fun, when you think about love, when you think about hugs, that's what AY exemplified."

And the winner? Hillman described the man, whose name is Bob Gelfond, as "truly an inspiration to a lot of people down here," and went on to describe how, fittingly given the name of the award and the circumstances, Gelfond had helped Young during the pitcher's battle against cancer, journeying to Young's house in Houston, personally assisting him and even footing some of Young's considerable medical bills.

Earning the Good Guy Award is not the only aspirational recognition conferred at the dinner. True to the fantasy effort to recreate the illusion of a major-league experience, Mets fantasy camp includes the ultimate sports accolade: election to a Hall of Fame. Like the real Baseball Hall of Fame, Mets Fantasy Camp Hall of Fame has its minimum entrance requirements: attend five consecutive fantasy camps, or seven non-consecutive, corresponding to the Cooperstown's 10-years-in-the majors minimum. And like the actual Hall of Fame, the remaining criteria are subjective and a player's election is very much at the whim of the selection committee: the Baseball Writers Association of America for the Cooperstown shrine and the previously selected inductees for the Port St. Lucie fantasy edition.

That self-selection places the Mets Fantasy Camp Hall of Fame closer in spirit to being elected to Cooperstown by the Veterans Committee. That panel was created to correct injustices by the writers, who had eschewed supporting a worthy candidate because of perceived grievances and slights ranging from off-field actions to general surliness with the media. But the Baseball Hall of Fame Veterans Committee's decisions opened themselves up to their own accusations of cronyism (demonstrated most graphically by the election of Bill Mazeroski to the Hall while keeping out Gil Hodges). And, at least among some of the Citi Slickers, the feeling is that the Mets Fantasy Hall of Fame operates in the same way.

Why, they wonder, have their teammates Phil Forman and Dave Helfrich, not been properly enshrined? Both have the requisite number of camps under their belts; both have put up numbers justifying selection; and both, at least the Citi Slickers believe, have made marks among their various teammates over the years to make them shoo-ins.

But, alas, once again this would not be either Forman or Helfrich's year.

Instead, three other campers are announced as the newest members of the club. Each gets the opportunity to address the group. The first, Bob Selski, notes that he has been to 13 camps, and thanks his wife. "She inspired me to come here," he says, immediately raising questions about the state of his marriage. "It's the best thing in the world."

The second is the most popular choice of the three. His name is Izzy Kushner and he is a human resources executive from New Jersey. His acceptance speech encapsulates the lure of a repeat fantasy camp experience: "You don't come here thinking you are going to make friends," he notes. "You come here to meet your idols, to meet those guys you've seen staying up late and night watching TV."

As he quickly notes, he has a somewhat unusual idol: Doug Flynn, the Gold Glove second baseman whose Mets career spanned about half of his 11-year MLB tenure and whose lifetime batting average of .238 with a mere seven home runs would not usually inspire idolatry. "I never told Doug this, but I wore number 23 [Flynn's Mets uniform number] until I was in college," Kushner says. "Doug Flynn was the guy. Imagine that's what you wanted to be?" The remark garners its expected laugh.

Back to the fantasy camp experience: "You come back, and people say, why do you come year in and year out? If you ever came, you'd know. They say you can't choose your family, but you know what, the day you sign up for Mets fantasy camp, you do."

That theme was echoed by the third, and most unusual selection: Wendy Shotsky, the first woman chosen for the Mets Fantasy Camp Hall of Fame. Shotsky, a New York State Department of Health employee, has been to 12 fantasy camps and in a 2015 interview with the *Albany Times-Union*, the local newspaper, would rank breaking up a fantasy camp no-hitter and starting he team's go-ahead rally as her biggest thrill-perhaps equal to, if not bigger, than the birth of her twins 37 years previously.

A Mets fan since the team's inception in 1962, Shotsky waxes biographical in her remarks. "I wanted to come to fantasy camp but my experience all my life was, you're a girl, you don't play baseball. I wanted to come to fantasy camp, but I was afraid to. I called them up and I said, 'Do you take women?' And they said, 'Sure, we take women.' I had never played baseball before. I wasn't allowed to play baseball. As a little girl, I didn't like softball .... but I desperately wanted to play baseball and so at the age of 57 I came here and played my first baseball game. I was terrible, but I was hooked, and I became part of the family here. I have never been treated with anything but kindness, love, and I've always been one of the guys."

What tangible benefit inures to the inductees? It would seem presumptuous to write "MFC HOF" after their autograph, but they do get their names engraved on a plaque and a patch sewn onto their uniform in succeeding years, which, at least in their minds, must make the minimum $25,000 buy-in (representing five years of costs) worthwhile. And they do get to vote for the future classes.

Their feelings about Forman and Helfrich were not disclosed.

The 2019 Mets Fantasy Camp Hall of Fame Inductees. (Photo courtesy of Marc Levine,Jennifer Voce-Nelson and Kayla Rice )

The program ends, somewhat disappointingly, with no rousing call to the campers to gather same time, next year after the champions receive their trophies and pose for their official championship photo. The campers begin milling about the ballroom for a final round of "see you at the reunion" (in May, at Citi Field in New York), and some final posed photos with the coaches.

Mark and Josh do not dally. Their cue for the week's end is a reported impending storm back in New York that has prompted them to switch travel arrangements, shaving a day off their Florida stay to ensure-especially necessary in Mark's case (one would assume that the Mets would be somewhat more understanding if Josh got stranded)-that they will make it back home in time to report to work the next Monday. Instead of easing out of camp, they need to arise early the next morning and drive back to the airport in West Palm Beach, about an hour away.

The next day, as their plane begins its descent into Long Island-MacArthur Airport to complete their return home, Mark looks out the window and sees the type of tableau Eric Hillman has described. He takes a photo, and then texts, the view of baseball fields, nine of them, at a Long Island complex-not quite as striking as an astronaut's photo from space, but striking and somewhat more symbolic.

Mark and Josh's final bonding experience has come to an end.

The end of an amazing experience. (Photo courtesy of Marc Levine,Jennifer Voce-
Nelson and Kayla Rice )

# CHAPTER 7
## EPILOGUE

Two days after returning from Mets Fantasy Camp, Mark was back at his job in Manhattan, planning the schedule of New York Rangers hockey games he would cover for the radio station and continuing to market his latest hockey book about the 1979 Rangers, which was published just before he left for Florida. In short, life was back to normal for him.

That same day, Josh was back at Citi Field, working alongside some of the same people who had chronicled his successes—and made sure to record his failures to become part of the office banter mill. Two weeks later, they would all trundle back to Port St. Lucie for spring training. The relationships were back to where they had been before he stepped out of his job and crossed over to the other side of the fence and became the subject of the videos and graphics instead of the instigator.

For Josh, the highlight of the week was spending a week with his father as peers instead of player and coach. "It was good to be on the other side after all those years of being coached to be able to kind of laugh and say, 'It isn't so easy, is it?'" Josh said, adding that his favorite part of the week came when coach Pete Schourek asked Mark if there was anything he hadn't done during the camp that he'd wanted to. "I was immediately able to say, 'Yeah, hit.' It was my way of giving back the tough love that maybe didn't get me to where I wanted to be as a baseball player but more so a man. I think what was better about the experience was how my dad was able to see how I am received by not just my coworkers but others around me. I was able to show him the type of man I have grown to be, which was important to me."

For Mark, the experience was worth the time and the expense. "I don't know if there is anyplace we could have spent an entire week like that together that would have come close to it," he said. And what was important to Josh was also important and moving to Mark, seeing how other people viewed his son. "Hearing Pete [Schourek] and Eric [Hillman] rave about what a special young man Josh was, even though it was something I already knew, was nice to hear from others," he said. "I remember walking back after the awards ceremonies and congratulating Josh on his Cleon Jones Award, I told him obviously I am proud of the award he won, but I was more impressed at the adult he had become."

Yes, Mark had some disappointments during the week, relating to his on-field performance. "But at the end of the day," he said, "I realized that I really didn't care about how I was doing. I was so busy watching and enjoying Josh play again."

Four months later, the fantasy campers gathered for a reunion before a Mets-Marlins game at Citi Field. Mark learned from Doug Dickey that 80 to 85 percent of the 2019 fantasy campers had already renewed for 2020.

Mark will not be one of them. "Not a chance in hell," Mark told Dickey, the fantasy camp director. "I explained it could never get better than this. If I came back solo, it just wouldn't be the same."

After all, some experiences truly are once in a lifetime and are best left that way.

# APPENDIX

## 240,000 WORDS

It's a scene that has been replayed thousands of times over the past 30 years as fans recall one of the seminal moments in baseball history: Mookie Wilson's slow roller somehow passing through Bill Buckner's legs and Ray Knight crossing home plate with the winning run in Game 6 of the 1986 World Series.

The immortal Vin Scully, calling the game on network television described the aftermath with ... silence. After a more than three-minute series of unnarrated flash cuts between stunned Red Sox and overjoyed Mets and their fans (Mark and his father among them), Scully broke the silence with:

"If one picture is worth a thousand words, you have seen about a million words."

With Scully's play on the adage in mind, what follows over the next few pages are 240,000 words.

When trying to come up with an idea for the back cover of this book, we reached out on social media, asking people to send photos of themselves with either their fathers or sons at major-league games.

We were inundated with images, so we decided to break the photos down by major-league team, select our starting nine of photos for each team, and include them as an appendix to the book instead of as the back cover.

Each photo is a story unto itself, whether it be the Houston Astros father and son recreating a pose decades apart, or a snapshot of the Baltimore Orioles son who got his love of the game via his dad's time as an usher at Memorial Stadium, or the multigenerational photos, or just the pure joy and smile that emanates from each face captured for prosperity as fathers and sons take in the game.

These are just a small sample size of the many photos submitted, feel free to leave yours on our Facebook page, **Glove Story: Fathers, Sons and the American Pastime.**

# ARIZONA DIAMONDBACKS

# ATLANTA BRAVES

# BALTIMORE ORIOLES

# BOSTON RED SOX

# CHICAGO WHITE SOX

# CHICAGO CUBS

# CINCINNATI REDS

# CLEVELAND INDIANS

# COLORADO ROCKIES

# DETROIT TIGERS

# HOUSTON ASTROS

# KANSAS CITY ROYALS

# LOS ANGELES ANGELS

# LOS ANGELES DODGERS

# MIAMI MARLINS

# MILWAUKEE BREWERS

# MINNESOTA TWINS

# NEW YORK YANKEES

# NEW YORK METS

# OAKLAND ATHLETICS

# PHILADELPHIA PHILLIES

Mark Rosenman and A.J. Carter

# PITTSBURGH PIRATES

# SAN DIEGO PADRES

# SAN FRANCISCO GIANTS

# SEATTLE MARINERS

# ST. LOUIS CARDINALS

# TAMPA BAY RAYS

# TEXAS RANGERS

# TORONTO BLUE JAYS

# WASHINGTON NATIONALS

# 2019 CITI SLICKERS

Front row from left to right Micth Waxman,Mark Rosenman, Josh Rosenman,
"Bobble" Ed Moore, Seth Davis, Back Row Pete Schourek, Bob Ghadi, David"Turtle"
Dolgin, Dwight'Doc" Gooden, Bob Whalen, Rich Boyd, David Helfrich, Eric Hillman,
(missing Phil Forman)
(Photo courtesy of Marc Levine,Jennifer Voce-Nelson and Kayla Rice)

# HOME TEAM

## THE ROSENMANS

Josh, Liana, Beth and Mark Rosenman (Photo courtesy of Mark Rosenman)

## THE CARTERS

From left to right: Elana Buckley,Doug, Eileen, Arnie and Evan Carter. (Photo courtesy of A.J. Carter)

Mark Rosenman and A.J. Carter